PATHWAYS TO
PRIVATE EQUITY
PARTNERSHIPS

BUILDING **GENERATIONAL WEALTH**
THROUGH **THEMATIC INVESTMENTS**

PATHWAYS TO
PRIVATE EQUITY PARTNERSHIPS

BUILDING **GENERATIONAL WEALTH**
THROUGH **THEMATIC INVESTMENTS**

PATRICK B. ROPELLA

Published in the USA by:

ROPELLA MEDIA

COPYRIGHT © 2024 PATRICK ROPELLA

All Rights Reserved

**THE PATHWAYS TO PRIVATE EQUITY PARTNERSHIPS
BUILDING GENERATIONAL WEALTH
THROUGH THEMATIC INVESTMENTS**

Paperback - ISBN: 9798327125544
Hardback - ISBN: 9798325931772

To my wife, best friend, and business partner of over 30 years, Robbie, thanks for keeping me humble, motivated, and focused on never, ever giving up.

To the Ropella 360 team members, past and present, for supporting, challenging, and teaching me how to be a better leader.

Together we grew one of the world's most respected executive search and PE consulting firms.

We worked hard, played hard, and along the way built an award-winning corporate culture.

To all the transformational leaders who retained us as clients, who trusted us with their careers, and supported us as vendors, creating countless friendships over the past 35 years.

We've learned a great deal of wisdom about how to grow great companies and lead great people, from many CEOs and investors much smarter than us.

And for all of you, we are eternally grateful.

How to open doors to opportunity?

First follow the 3 Cs:

Character, Competence, and Cost

This is what gets you through the door.

(Cost is what you're willing to personally invest. It equals your own Time, Talent, and Treasure).

Now that you've gotten through the door...

What keeps you at the conference table?

It's all about ACTION leadership:

Accountability, Communication, and Trust

How you A.C.T. is what makes relationships last, especially under pressure.

Leaders are like eagles.

They don't flock, you find them one at a time.

Like is short, so wherever you are:

Be there, be focused, and be present.

Contents

Introduction **1**

PART ONE: UNDERSTANDING THE WORLD OF PRIVATE EQUITY (PE)

Chapter One:
An Overview of How PE Firms Differentiate Themselves **8**

Chapter Two:
The Typical Roles Within and/or Supporting a PE Firm **18**

Chapter Three:
How To Get Access to Key Leadership at a PE Firm **30**

PART TWO: FINDING THE RIGHT PE PARTNER

Chapter Four:
Screening the Right PE Firms to Consider Working With....................**38**

Chapter Five:
Scoring the Right PE Firms With Which You're Interviewing...........**44**

PART THREE: DEVELOPING THE PE PARTNERSHIP STRATEGY

Chapter Six:
Before You Start Racing with PE, Develop a Winning Strategy......**48**

Chapter Seven:
Executing Your PE Race Strategy with Goals and Timetables...........**55**

Chapter Eight:
Compensation and Incentivization While Creating Generational Wealth **67**

Acknowledgments **82**

About The Author **83**

Introduction

Throughout this book, Family Offices (FO) and Private Equity (PE) firms will be referenced as PE. The explanations and content provided throughout apply equally to PE firms and those FOs that are already managing or striving to manage their investment platforms like PE firms.

You might be surprised to learn how many different paths there are to developing working relationships with PE and FO investment firms. There are so many other roles, titles, and opportunities working within and supporting the different types of PE firms that most people have very little idea of what they all are.

Through hundreds of interviews on this topic, I've learned that most executives have little knowledge of what goes on behind the closed "secretive doors" of private equity. Often, the executives I speak with have an inkling based on the limited perspective/lenses they have obtained through working for one or two PE-owned companies, or through the limited perspective/lenses they have obtained from selling one or two companies to PE firms.

Throughout this book, when I use the term "executives," understand we are mostly speaking to C-Suite leaders (commonly referred to as CXOs) and the board members who support them. If you're not at that level yet… no harm, no foul. This book can still be a helpful tool. Learn what you need to know now so you will be much better equipped to partner successfully with PE leadership when you are at the C-Suite level.

This book is written for three primary audiences:

1. The founders/CEOs who are selling their business to a PE firm.
2. The CXOs looking to make a career shift into the world of PE.
3. PE firms that want to learn best practices to recruit great leadership from the first two camps.

Often, this is the scenario for the first audience…

Over the past few years, you've received multiple calls from PE firms, investment bankers, and sell-side advisors. Your peers, accountant, and lawyer have recommended that you take those calls and have those discussions. Your business is successful, you're prepared financially for retirement, and you're looking at your company's succession plan, and wondering...What's next? You don't know much about succession planning, exit planning, or even how to evaluate which PE firm you should be considering. Moreover, selling your company to a PE firm seems like an obvious path for you to invest your valuable time. That said, you've seen some peers do well with this approach... while others say it's been a total nightmare. So, where do you start? You might be thinking: Maybe I should just give the business to my children or employees. The biggest question on your mind is: How do I get my wealth out of the business now while I'm still healthy enough to enjoy it?

Often, this is the scenario for the second audience...

You're an upper-level career executive. You've had a good run so far, and now you're getting regular calls from headhunters looking for CXOs for PE-backed companies. You've seen peers switch from corporate and publicly owned companies to PE firms. So now you're wondering what it might be like for you to work for a PE-backed company and if the PE world is indeed the next path for you. You're thinking: How do I evaluate which PE firms fit my style and ambitions? You've heard scary things from peers who say it's a dramatically different world, demands are higher, and patience levels are shorter. How do you know if you can manage in this environment? You've also heard that PE can be risky but total compensation can be much greater... so how does that all work?

Don't assume you're fully prepared, whether you're coming from the first audience or the second.

Selling your company to a PE firm can be a daunting task. There are significant financial reasons why having competent and experienced advisors can make the difference between having just a good sale versus having a great sale experience. Preparing financials well in advance, top-grading key leadership roles, polishing up the day-to-day business processes, making facility improvements, and creating the presentations for prospective investors takes a lot of time and everything needs to be well thought through.

Entering the world of PE through a career shift is equally challenging, similar to a professional athlete attempting to shift from one sport to another. The playing field for a CXO in corporate America is entirely different compared to working within or supporting a PE firm. The rules and players differ completely from one firm (or team) to the next.

But don't worry. I'm here to be your guide. I look forward to coaching you, and helping you learn the rules and how to avoid the penalties. I want you to enter the arena with confidence, and I want you to win.

As your coach, it's worth knowing my background. The Ropella 360 team and I have a combined 25 years of success working with PE firms all over the globe. We've partnered effectively with hundreds of PE leaders in a wide variety of ways. These experiences, "learning through the school of hard knocks," through trial and error, have seasoned us well, and now we are happy to share our experience and wisdom on the following pages.

So, relax and enjoy the read. Once you've completed this book, you will have an excellent understanding of the wide and various paths to PE success, and how to choose the one that's best for you. We'll help you prepare to step confidently onto the field of PE — ready to play your best.

When I interview executives and ask them this question: "What opportunities or roles are you aware of within PE firms where you could partner?" This is what I hear the most:

- We can sell our company to a PE firm.
- I can become a CEO... through a PE firm for one of their holdings.
- I can get a board seat... through a PE firm for one of their holdings.

or I hear a combination of these three options.

These are only three typical responses compared to a dozen possible paths for how an executive can become a valuable consultant, member, or partner within a PE Firm.

It's interesting, and sometimes even funny (even when asking leaders within PE firms) how often I only get three to four (out of the dozen) paths back as a response to that question. For example, when I ask, "What roles or opportunities are you aware of within your PE firm where executives could partner with you?" most have limited perspectives, based on their limited lenses, in their unique focus on PE.

Ropella 360 has spoken with thousands of PE leaders and executives who have personally partnered directly with PE, and has developed a comprehensive list of the most typical paths to successfully partnering with PE:

1. **Sell your company to a PE firm.**
2. **Serve as an industry subject matter expert (SME) in an hour-long phone interview for a PE leader.**

3. Serve as a River Guide and consult on an industry thesis for one to three months for a PE leader.
4. Serve as a Due Diligence/SME Advisor during an acquisition, addressing special topics for a PE leader.
5. Serve as a Backable Executive on acquisition hunting for Platform(s) and/or Bolt-On(s) for a PE leader.
6. Serve as a Serial Acquisition Hunter and find multiple Platforms and then multiple Bolt-Ons, as a career focus for a PE firm (not just the one PE leader).
7. Serve as a Board Member over a PE firm's corporate holding(s).
8. Serve as a part-time Executive Chairman over a PE firm's corporate holding(s).
9. Become a full-time employee of a PE firm as an Operating Advisor in support of a PE firm's corporate holding(s).
10. Become a full-time Principal/ VP/Fundraiser or Partner within a PE firm.
11. Become an independent Business Development Acquisition "Lead Generator" for a list of PE and other investment firms.
12. Serve in an administrative role (over Human Resources, Accounting, Marketing, Finance, IT, etc.) in a PE firm.
13. Start your own PE (Venture Capital or FO) firm.

Now that you've seen all the paths, how do you select the right one? Not so fast! Next, you need to understand that there are different types of PE firms with different cultures and investment models.

It's true — it used to be much easier to understand PE firms. All you had to do was read the book *Barbarians at the Gate* or watch the *Pretty Woman* movie, and you'd have the impression that all PE firms are sharks — crazy aggressive, neurotic, and with leaders who only care about making tons of money at the expense of the people who worked (often their whole lives) for the acquired companies.

Often, we hear, "I know all about PE because of this story or that experience." Well, how long ago was that story or experience? And how many stories or experiences related to different PE firms have you heard of or had? The point is that private equity is a burgeoning industry that continues to expand and change at a very rapid pace.

The PE community has evolved dramatically from its beginnings roughly more than 40 years ago. In 1990, it was estimated that there were just over 300 PE firms. Now, there are thousands of PE firms across the globe, all competing for funding, the best talent, and most importantly, good press. Often, the way leadership treats and even builds relationships with those affected by PE firm transactions is now a significant focus of pride for most PE firms. It didn't used to be that way, but it's worth realizing that things do change.

This steeper learning and faster growth curve in the PE industry has forced differentiation among PE firms. Differentiation is now required to make PE firms "stand out" when raising funds, attracting top talent, and/or targeting sellers to make acquisitions. The best PE firms are clearly and carefully spelling out their unique, compelling attributes in increasingly creative, marketing-driven ways.

Whether you are a business founder/owner looking to sell your business or an executive looking to partner with a PE firm as part of a career transition, you need to understand all these differences before learning which fit would be the most rewarding for you and your ambitions.

In this book, we will help you select and navigate your chosen course. For almost 40 years, Ropella 360 has been advising senior leaders within Fortune 500 and larger global corporations, inside mid-market companies, and even startups. We have been serving as super-connectors to bring the best people, often referred to as "A-players" and the most successful, transformational leaders, to the conference table, with the goal of helping them grow their great companies and careers.

Our primary role has been helping corporate leaders make the right hires, selecting A-players and transformational "Level 5 Leaders" who can take their companies from Good to Great. We are now successfully doing the same for PE firms.

Whether it's solving searches for mid- and senior-level executives or C-Suite leaders and board members, the key is that the right people, hired at the right time, still make the greatest difference in any organization's success.

This also applies to great people choosing which organization they will join next. It's crucial for these new hires to make the right decision and find the best fit to further their career and personal ambitions.

As you read this book, it's important for you to understand that partnering with

PE is all about obtaining success and, ideally, achieving it fast. PE firms do not tolerate foolishness or wasted time and they typically move very smart and very fast. Pitching your skill set, passions, and goals to the wrong firm can prove to be a massive frustration for everyone involved and can be a waste of your own time too.

This book is written to ensure that you effectively consider which PE firm is the ideal "right fit" for you to support, work for, and/or to make an investment with. In the following pages, we'll show you how to leverage your past skills, experiences, special industry knowledge, personality, available time, talent, and treasure once you select the right PE firm with which to partner.

Over the past five years, Ropella 360 has hyper-focused its business development efforts to the point of almost exclusively serving PE firms, conducting searches for a wide variety of leaders, and sourcing leads for buying and selling businesses. As a result, we have developed thousands of global relationships with Founders, Partners, and key leaders at hundreds of PE, Venture Capital (VC), and FO investment firms.

We now know firsthand, through hundreds of clients we've served, that organically scaling up a business and adding acquisitions is no small feat. As my favorite CEO Coach, Verne Harnish, teaches, it's all about Scaling Up through PEOPLE, STRATEGY, EXECUTION, and CASH.

That being said, as Jim Collins (from his best-selling book Good to Great) teaches, it all starts with getting "the right people on the bus, and the right people in the right seats."

It's not surprising that 80% of all great leadership books clearly state that hiring the RIGHT people (A-players and Level 5 Transformational Leaders) makes the greatest difference. It's as simple as it sounds — be the best and then find the best people to partner with, because this is the fastest path to scale up while going from good to great.

Here's hoping that this book makes it happen for you.

www.ropella360.com

PART ONE

UNDERSTANDING THE WORLD OF PRIVATE EQUITY (PE)

Chapter One: An Overview of How PE Firms Differentiate Themselves

To help you fully understand the world of PE and how PE firms differentiate themselves, let's take a page from a Journalism 101 textbook and use "The 5 Ws and the H" method to explore the world of PE:

- **Who** are they?
- **What** do they do?
- **When** do they do it?
- **Where** do they do it?
- **How** do they do it?
- **Why** do they do it?

> **FOOD FOR THOUGHT ON BUILDING A PROFESSIONAL ADVISORY TEAM**
>
> This book is not intended to provide investment advice or financial counseling. We do not steer our clients with legal, tax, or accounting advice. Rather, we strongly encourage you to build your own subject matter expert (SME) team of legal, tax, accounting, and/or investment banking advisors.
>
> The outcomes of any investment transactions in which you get involved will be impacted by a wide variety of laws, rules, and regulations — federal, state, and/or local. How you interpret and make decisions will depend on facts you and your advisors will need to fully comprehend. Now is not the time to be penny-wise and pound-foolish. Trying to "save" by scrimping on your advisory team is not the way to go.

Who they are:

Let's start by defining a PE fund. A PE fund aggregates or combines money from various investors and pools that money into a single fund. The people or entities investing in a PE fund are called Limited Partners (LPs). The LPs investing in a fund are usually high-net-worth individuals and/or families, companies, organizations, countries, or pension funds. Funds typically have a minimum investment, say for example, $5 million. The PE firm then uses the combined funds ($100 Million to $3 Billion) to purchase or acquire a controlling stake in multiple companies.

LPs have no decision-making authority over the PE firm or the investments made by the fund. The PE firm serves as the General Partner over the legal entity of the named fund and has total control over the use of funds and investments.

The LPs make financial commitments by pledging capital for a specified period, generally for the life of the fund, and, unlike publicly traded shares of stock, do not buy and sell at any time. In other words, there's little to no liquidity until the fund's charter expires. Some funds are set to expire in 5 years, most in 10 years, and it's common to have built-in extensions for an extra year or two. PE firms start investing by issuing capital calls to the committed LPs to collect the money needed. Larger PE firms have multiple and overlapping funds. Some late-stage and some early-stage PE firms operate with dozens of holdings or portfolio companies acquired with these funds.

The life span of each fund will depend on various factors determined by the type and size of the investments and each fund's charter that directs the LP agreements. As anchor or platform acquisitions are made and bolt-ons are connected and sold (typically within a 5-year average from buy to sell time), investors receive distributions and possibly make additional commitments to invest into the same PE firm's next/new funds.

There are reporting requirements to communicate to the LPs during the fund's life. Quarterly financial reports, serving much like scorecards, are sent out to discuss the funds, where the monies have been invested, what returns have been distributed, and the current opinion of the value of invested funds.

Annual meetings with the LPs are conducted to provide an update on the status of existing holdings and current acquisition targets. To encourage attendance at these meetings, high-profile guest speakers, such as the CEOs of the holdings and/or subject matter experts guiding acquisition hunting activities, may be invited.

All PE firms work to differentiate themselves and attract the attention of the limited pool of LP capital investors. The most common PE focus is on the size of the acquisitions the firm is targeting, which also typically correlates closely to the life cycle of a target company.

Let's first look at the investment size of acquisition targets, which is based on revenue, then earnings before interest, taxes, depreciation, and amortization (EBITDA — pronounced e-bit-dah), and debt... or the size of the check required to make an acquisition.

In simplistic terms, there are typically three PE firm sizes: small, medium, and large:

1. **Small PE Firms**
   - Typically acquire small to lower-middle-market-sized businesses.
   - They typically operate one fund at a time and won't start a second fundraise until 70% of the funds from the first fund have been deployed.
   - They typically have a home base of operations in one location.

2. **Medium PE Firms**
   - Typically acquire businesses in the lower-middle-market to upper-middle-market ranges.
   - They typically have three to five funds operating at the same time.
   - They typically have a home base of operations in one location, with a handful of satellite locations around the country where they are based.

3. **Large PE Firms**
   - Typically acquire upper-middle-market to very large-sized businesses.
   - They have hundreds of employees and typically ten or more funds operating simultaneously.
   - They typically have offices in locations across the globe.

Now let's look at the stages during which companies typically take on investors:

- **Startup/IP Development Stage:** Almost exclusively funded by family and friends, banks, angel investors, and VC firms.
- **Commercialization Stage:** The business is growing, but revenue and EBITDA are below the typical threshold of most PE firms' investment strategies ($10 million in revenue and $2 million in EBITDA). These companies are typically funded by banks, angel investors, VC firms, FOs,

and some small PE firms.

- **Scaling-Up Stage:** The business is now considered mature and stable, and revenue and EBITDA now meet the threshold of most PE firms' investment strategies. At this point, a group of PE firms, FOs, and strategic acquirers may be interested in looking at this business. The business is now typically past the stage of requesting funding from Family and Friends, Angel Investors, and VC firms. The business has a clear path to sustainable growth through organic initiatives and M&A.

There is a fourth stage of business growth — what is sometimes referred to as the **"Elephant Stage."** These are typically well-established, Fortune 500 or larger global companies or incredibly fast-growing speculative software, social media, or AI companies — but these are not the focus of this book. These companies are typically funded on publicly traded stock exchanges by very large institutional investors or ultra-high-net-worth individual investors. They are not typical of most PE investment firms.

Common fund types:

Buyout Fund

This is the most common and well-known type of PE fund, and is the primary focus of this book. A Buyout Fund purchases controlling stakes in companies. Majority ownership is the norm, and the fund typically includes more mature and well-established companies with minimum revenues of $10 million and $1-$2 million in EBITDA.

Venture Capital Fund

VC funds make small, minority-stake investments in early-stage emerging businesses. Typically, the existing CEO retains most of the day-to-day control over these investments. Here, investing in ideas with solid potential is the norm. Revenue is often minimal to none… but there's great promise for fast growth.

Fund of Funds

Much like a stand-alone mutual fund, the General Partner takes money from a wide range of investors and invests it in other PE funds. This allows for more diversification and allows investors to invest in a larger "pool of PE funds."

Debt Funds

Some larger PE firms will have private debt funds to loan to other PE-backed portfolio companies. Due to conflicts of interest, they rarely lend to their holdings.

Instead of companies or PE firms paying the banks interest on loans, these funds earn the interest for themselves. Used as part of leveraged debt for acquiring companies or growing companies through credit lines, this is typically seen as minimal risk — a rewarding way to provide diversification to the PE firm's LPs.

Pooled/Co-Investing Funds

Often, PE firms co-invest with other PE firms. When an acquisition opportunity is larger than their fund typically allows for or they want to spread the risk, they will have one PE firm take a controlling interest and the other a minority interest in the investment.

LP/Co-Investments

Often, to reward an operating advisor, board member, acquisition hunter, or a management team, a PE firm will team with individuals on a separate investment. This is often designed to get more active supporters of the acquisition to put more "skin in the game."

What they do:

Once the PE firm justifies its capital call by finding an acquisition and completing due diligence, it purchases the company based on the amount of EBITDA agreed to times a multiplication factor of X. This determines the purchase price.

The **multiplication factor** (abbreviated as MF and often referred to as the "multiple") is determined based on a wide variety of factors. Like past related industry transactions (just like appraisal opinions are formed for real estate values), the value of property, inventories and other tangible assets. As well, brand value, intellectual property value, debt levels, customer concentration and longevity. Also, revenue consistency and growth, diversification of business lanes, and the realistic nature of a robust growth plan are taken into account as part of determining the MF.

Consideration is also given to the quality of the leadership team, how long the key leaders will remain involved post-sale, and the quality of processes, systems, and procedures in place (HR, accounting, IT, purchasing, etc.). Based on the opinion of value, the MF goes up and down until all parties agree that it is fair, balanced, and worth agreeing upon.

For example, let's say the due diligence process is completed and has determined (with the buying and selling parties agreement) that a food ingredients business is producing $5 million in annual EBITDA.

All parties agree, that the MF should range from 7 to 10 based on similar food ingredients businesses. Negotiations result in an agreement that the MF will be applied as 8. So, $5 million in EBITDA x 8 dictates an enterprise value (EV) of $40 million.

First, the PE firm will use debt financing, the maximum amount of leverage or debt that can be managed based on the cash flow the company can allow. Second, a capital call will be made to cover the balance of the purchase price and funding needed to scale up the business. Based on each LP's percentage of commitment to the fund — and the dollar amount needed to be raised — a proportional check will be requested of each LP.

As a basic example, a $40 million EV acquisition is reduced to a $20 million capital call with $20 million financed through debt. The LPs combined capital calls can make up 100% of the fund commitments. In this case, let's say one of the LPs is a police pension fund that has committed 10% of the fund... so 10% of $20 million means $2 million will be the police pension funds capital call investment.

When they do it:

Investment Timeline Focus:

Capital returns to the LPs over time. When a PE firm sells one of its companies and holdings or refinances to create distributions, it returns capital to its LPs.

Using the same food ingredients business example as above — let's say the company is sold five years later, following solid growth in revenue and EBITDA. Instead of the EBITDA being $5 million as it was at the time of acquisition, it is now $15 million. Earnings increased three times over the 5 years.

The company is now considered even stronger across many measures, and a large strategic buyer (typically a competitor) has agreed that the MF will be 10X. The current $15 million in EBITDA times an MF of 10 creates an enterprise value of $150 million. Considering the business was acquired for $40 million five years ago, and it's now sold for $150 million, the result is a gain of $110 million... so the investors are all happy.

Now, the $150 million needs to be shared with the investors, but first, the $20 million in debt financing needs to be paid off. The firm has also added an additional $20 million in debt and transaction fees by buying two other bolt-ons connected to the original platform acquisition (the first food ingredients business).

Combining the debt, legal and accounting fees, investment banker fees, consulting fees, carried interest fees, etc. of $40 million (for a simple math example), the distribution math now works like this:

$150 million minus $40 million ($20 million in original debt + $20 million in additional debt and transaction fees) = $110 million for distribution back to the LPs.

As a 10% LP, the police pension fund now receives $11 million on its original $2 million investment. This investment performance could be described at a Multiple of Invested Capital (MOIC) of 5.5.

Where they do their investing:

Geographic Focus:

Where PE firms make their investments often depends on the firm's size.

- **Small PE firms** typically focus on local to regional investments. It's easier to manage relationships with the leadership you have managing your holdings when they are close at hand. As well, when you're a small firm with limited time and resources to spend chasing leads and conducting meetings nationwide or even globally, this drives location factors.

- **Mid-sized and large PE firms** focus nationally and/or globally. With technology (Microsoft Teams or Zoom and shared presentation capabilities), the barriers to working long distances at any time of the day have never been lower. And larger teams have more associates to help with preparations, travel, lightening the load for the senior leadership in the PE firm.

Industry Focus:

- **Small PE firms** tend to stay in one or two specific industry lanes. A small firm with an executive serving as the firm's founder or senior partner who comes from the chemical industry is likely to stay focused on what that person knows best. For example, chemical acquisition targets. Over time, founders and their partners will spread their wings and look at closely related adjacencies or "allied industries" such as coatings, cosmetics, plastics, etc. Over time, they may create a third lane for "not elsewhere classified (NEC)" acquisition interests, or a broad, generalized, catch-all buckets called business services or general industrials.

- **Mid-sized and large PE firms** typically have a core industry focus plus three to five secondary core industry lanes on which they focus the most — then a few catch-all buckets for everything else.

Most PE firms do a good job of clearly spelling out where they focus as a firm, and it's right there for all to see on their website. Then, you get into phone or face-to-face discussions with the PE firm, and their annually updated presentation decks are opened. During presentations, they draw even greater clarity on what they are most focused on now — with a forward-looking statement typically covering the next year.

How they make money:

When you invest in mutual funds, management fees are described up front and applied to your investments. The same applies to PE funds. The typical management fee of a PE fund is 2%, which is designed to cover overhead — not specifically to generate wealth for the PE firm. The primary tool a PE firm uses to generate wealth is referred to as "carried interest."

Limited partners typically pay back 20% on every dollar of profit they earn from the PE firm. As described with the police pension fund example, a $2 million investment became worth $9.5 million. So, at 20% of $11 million, the PE firm earned a commission of $2.2 million from the police pension fund.

The PE firm founders also make money, as the partners and senior leadership often invest in their own funds. This aligns with the LP's interests, too, as they want skin in the game for the PE investors in which they are investing. When PE leaders invest directly in the companies they are acquiring, they create a sub-fund to do so.

Now, it's important to know that making money is one thing, but raising more money — so you can launch more funds and then repeat the investment process — is quite another. Some firms and their funds perform better than others. To help investors compare, there are metrics for each PE fund — similar to Morningstar's reported metrics for mutual funds.

There are five PE fund rankings, with three carrying a little more weight than the others:

1. **Quartile-based -** A **GREAT** fund is in the top 25% quartile. A **GOOD** fund is in the 25 to 50% quartile. An **AVERAGE** fund is in the 50 to 75% quartile. A **BELOW AVERAGE** fund is in the bottom 25% quartile.
2. **Vintage-based -** The year a fund makes its first investment establishes its vintage year. Applying this ranking allows for the isolation of general economic trends that may have impacted the performance of all funds

during this period. This is how you compare fund performance on an "apples-to-apples" basis.

3. **Internal Rate of Return (IRR)-based** - This is considered the most important ranking. It is the net return earned by LPs over a particular period expressed as a percentage, taking into account the time value of money. A **GREAT** IRR is typically around 20%. A **GOOD** IRR is typically around 15%.

4. **Multiple on Invested Capital (MOIC)-based** - This is the net cash return divided by the initial capital investment. The primary difference between IRR and MOIC is that MOIC does not consider the time value of money. Nonetheless, they both are worthy measurements. A good MOIC may land in the range of 2X to 3X but will vary by asset and industry.

5. **Distributions to be Paid in Capital (DPI)-based** - This measures the ratio of money the fund distributes against the total amount invested into the fund (at any point during the fund's life). At the beginning of a fund, DPI stands at zero. The fund breaks even with a DPI of one as distributions are made. In an active fund, the DPI shows the velocity of how fast the fund returns money to shareholders. DPIs will vary extensively, but a DPI of 1.5 or more is generally considered "good" at the end of a fund's life.

These five rankings are interrelated. LPs use these rankings to form opinions about the PE firm and how their funds are performing now and in the past.

If you are a founder or CEO selling a company to a PE firm, especially if you have multiple PE firms from which to choose, or an executive or CEO considering partnering with a PE firm, don't hesitate to ask these firms for their rankings. You'll learn a whole lot about the firm and its leadership by asking. Also, simply requesting this information can paint you in a whole new light by the PE leaders with whom you interact.

Why they are investing:

The above-described PE firm income-generation model has become exceedingly popular because it is extremely successful, thereby fueling the massive growth of the number of PE firms across the planet. This is also why more than 50% of all mergers and acquisitions in the U.S. are now completed by PE firms, whereas 20 years ago, it was about 10% and 40 years ago, it was only 1%.

PE firms typically beat most stock benchmark indices. Yes, there's risk in PE investing, but arguably no more than investing in the Nasdaq or the S&P 500.

The level of due diligence that goes into every acquisition is typically extensive, with multiple experts involved, and the models for applying due diligence are well-tested, highly practiced, and constantly refined. Some would even argue that PE investing is less risky than investing in publicly traded stocks.

Understanding the risks of investing is the key to making sound financial decisions and wise investments. PE leaders are some of the best investigators and investment decision-makers on the planet. Highly experienced PE leaders, especially at middle to large PE firms, often come from CEO roles where they have been highly successful industry leaders. In addition, many executives have often been involved in businesses at all four stages (from Startups to Elephants).

Getting a seat at the table and sitting next to these high-caliber leaders is a once-in-a-lifetime opportunity for most executives. Learning how to get through their doors is valuable, and more importantly, learning how to keep a seat at their conference room table is priceless.

For you... this is exactly why I drafted this book!

> "Waiting helps you as an investor and a lot of people just can't stand to wait. If you didn't get the deferred-gratification gene, you've got to work very hard to overcome that."
>
> –Charlie Munger

Chapter Two: The Typical Roles Within and/or Supporting a PE Firm

It's important to have a good understanding of the typical roles within a PE firm before you walk into their office. Knowing these roles will help you understand who's on first, who's on second, and who is there to help you, as you need resources and solutions. The infographic below gives you a sense of who works inside the PE firm as a paid team vs. those who support the PE firm as external vendors or paid consultants.

External Support	Internal Support
River Guide • Industry Advisors	Operating & Managing Partners
Backable Executive	Active Chairman • Exec. Chairman
Serial Acquisition Hunter	• CEO Coach
Due Diligence SME Consultants	Board Member • Advisor • Chair

Additional PE Team Member Roles
Disclaimer: Additional PE Team Member Roles are all internal support.

| Founder(s)
Fund Raising
Investor Relations
Partners
Managing Directors | Ops Admin:
Bus Dev., HR, IT,
Fin., Legal & Res | Investment Staff:
Principal • VP •
Associate • Analyst |

The most senior role is that of founder. Alongside, or just below, is that of partner or, interchangeably, managing director.

Like the Formula 1 racing teams, they are the owners and general managers of the team. These PE leaders have the most tenure — typically in a smaller firm, 10 or more years, and at larger firms, 20 or more years of experience. They've cut their teeth on the climb up as CEOs and/or have worked at large investment firms, and they are now the key deal brokers, strategy makers, and the best negotiators. They interface directly with the CEOs of the PE-backed companies and their board members. They control all high-level decisions — key hiring and firing decisions, investment decisions, and the final decisions when it's time to sell investment holdings.

These people are supported by investment and management committees and will report back to them on how to ensure accountability flows both ways.

At the mid-level, the player's titles are principals or vice presidents.

Using the Formula 1 race team analogy again, these people function like special coaches, managing the connection to investors, the builders of the cars, the analysts tracking the race statistics, the mechanic team, and the pit crews. These PE roles serve as supporters or consultants to the CEOs. They provide information but typically do not give directions to CEOs. They provide day-to-day oversight for the portfolio companies, actively collaborating with them and doing heavy lifting on special projects — but not directing strategy nor making key decisions. Data and numbers are valuable to the scaling-up process. These people are instrumental in collecting, organizing, and reporting this data back to the partner.

The junior-level players are titled associates and analysts.

These are the race team's crew. These roles comprise the PE firm's teams of scouts, statisticians, and number crunchers. Typically, these people are in their 20s and right out of top-tier undergraduate programs — often with a master's degree and/or an MBA. These are high-potential future VPs and/or principals who must earn their stripes. They often work 60 to 80 hours a week on massive data collection and analysis projects.

They don't often have much, if any, exposure to the CEO, occasionally interfacing with the CFO and/or controllers and those who report to the other C-Suite leaders, like the directors and VPs. Their role is to answer questions about what's happening in the industry, analyze trends, and look at competitive comparisons. For example, how would a recession likely affect this kind of holding, or how does a strong economy present a growth opportunity for a particular type of investment? Their role also involves helping build investment models to determine how much a PE firm might offer a company for purchase or how much it might ask when selling a company.

For every 50 companies a PE firm considers, it might only make an offer to purchase one of them. These analysts won't make a buy or sell decision and won't be involved in negotiating a purchase. Still, their data collection and analysis during the initial diligence phases often uncover why so many acquisition opportunities are rejected. So don't take their contributions for granted, as their data and analysis sway many PE leaders' decisions.

In the introduction section of this book, I listed 13 ways you can interact with or support PE firms. Here, I'll provide a high-level overview of each path.

1. Sell your company to a PE firm.

There are several ways to sell your company. One of the more popular ways is to use an investment banker or sell-side broker. The key to selecting the right banker or broker is finding one that has an extensive Rolodex of contacts in your specific industry lane. As their plan A, they should know who to call at your competitors and/or customers — as these strategic buyers are typically the best place to start if you want to get maximum value for your sale.

Then, as part of their plan B, they should know who to call at the PE firms that are investing in your direct competitors. Many online resources help you find these investment bankers and sell-side brokers. Ropella 360 is one of them. If we can help in any way, don't hesitate to call.

As a CEO, COO, OR CFO, one of the first resources we will suggest you read in preparation for selling your company is the book Backable by Suneel Gupta, with the subtitle: T*he Surprising Truth Behind What Makes People Take a Chance on You.* The book teaches and then helps you complete a process for mentally and organizationally preparing to raise funds to grow your company, find a buyer to purchase your company, or get financial backing for just about any venture in which you're involved.

How well you communicate and sell yourself makes a massive difference in how much money you raise or what price you get at a sale. It's one thing to sell your products or services — and you're probably great at this. It's another thing to sell yourself in a job interview - and you wouldn't be where you are now if you hadn't proven your competency here as well. That said, it's a whole new level of lift — heavier and higher — to sell yourself when raising funds. Most corporate executives are not great or highly practiced at doing this work, which often occurs in front of strangers. Backable is a terrific book that helps you understand what sophisticated investors look for and how to differentiate yourself in their eyes and hearts.

2. **Serve as an industry subject matter expert (SME) in an hour-long phone interview for a PE leader.**

Gerson Lehrman Group (GLG) is a financial and global information services company. The company provides investors, consultants, and business clients who are seeking expert advice with the world's largest expert network - with more than one million freelance consultants serving as SMEs in every industry and topic imaginable. For $1,000, they will connect a PE investor or business leader client with an SME. The client gets charged, and the SME gets paid to have an hour-long conversation to answer a list of questions related to the SME's specific set of skills and experiences.

3. **Serve as a River Guide and consult on an industry thesis for one to three months for a PE leader:**

River Guides help PE firms and investors understand and navigate an industry segment at the highest levels. Then, additional investments can help drill down into market niches within the industry segment. If you're an investor who wants to understand an industry segment or, more specifically, a market niche in which you have little to no experience, River Guides (sometimes called Swamp Guides) can be extremely valuable to help you reduce learning time, avoid wasted time chasing rabbits, and even help you understand the dangers lurking in unknown waters.

Companies such as Apex Leaders and Bluewave take the above hour-long phone interview (as provided by GLG) to the next level and provide a deeper "expert search" connection. They both offer introductory services to help investors find River Guides — typically industry generalists versus specific niche specialists — to work on a billable-hour basis to help investors build out a draft thesis that can lead to an acquisition strategy. A thesis is just another word in the corporate world for building a business plan, or in the applicable vernacular of an investor, the first step towards building a strategic plan for targeting acquisitions. This approach is more valuable than just an hour-long exploratory discussion about an industry.

Ropella 360 takes this expert search approach to the next level. We apply a hyper-focused executive search model to target the right companies and individuals with very specific search parameters. We target individuals with the correct titles at these researched and targeted companies and consulting firms. We then comprehensively recruit and carefully screen prospects against a list of must-have skills and experiences. We are screening for extremely specific expertise, conflict-free, available bandwidth, and will fit your and the PE Firm's timetable. We will also screen for the gravitas and communications skills that set them apart as highly effective "prospctive" acquisition hunters.

We then schedule a formal interview process for a full slate of these SME candidates, often a half dozen or more — versus typically just one or two. Our slate of options is confirmed as highly relevant to the industry segment and the market niche our client is most interested in investing in, and better yet, our slate is confirmed as connected to the leadership at the target companies that the investor would like to potentially acquire.

We then partner with the investor to help them select the absolute best person within the slate of options for the specific industry.

If you are interested in being a candidate on our "radar"— or are an investor interested in this highly unique service offering, please don't hesitate to contact us at **www.ropella360.com**.

4. **Serve as a Due Diligence (DD)/SME Advisor during an acquisition, addressing special topics for a PE leader:**

What's the difference between a River Guide and a DD/SME Advisor? Honestly, not a whole lot. It's just the next step in the process of evaluating acquisition prospects. First, the River Guide sets the acquisition strategy as part of building out a draft thesis. Then the PE firm, using its business development team or an Acquisition Hunter's help (often with a supporting vendor like Ropella 360) chases down acquisition prospects to generate viable leads.

Once a viable acquisition lead has surfaced, questions are raised, and often, concerns and/or uncertainties about the viability of the acquisition come to light. The PE leaders then bring in the DD/SME Advisors to help flush out answers, solutions, and/or recommendations for the next steps.

Typically, the same people who provided an hour-long industry overview or helped with the building of the thesis are good candidates to address DD issues. This can work, but typically, it doesn't get you far down the river or very well-educated. Often, the more valuable DD topic is centered on a specific question about a financial, digital, HR, supply chain, R&D, QC, regulatory, marketing, sales, geography, or some other specific scaling-up issue.

In this case, getting an opinion from an industry expert is considered valuable, but a person who has worked for a direct competitor or a customer of the acquisition target could provide even greater insight. This is what the wisest PE firm leaders desire most. So, keep in mind that the most valuable DD/SME advisor also has specific, deep expertise in the functional issue or question being raised.

For example, our PE client says they need a food industry expert who understands the "niche ingredients used in making foods last longer on the shelf," and can provide insight about expanding the market for these products beyond domestic shores into Asia. The more specific the issue, the more valuable it is to find the right DD/SME advisor.

5. **Serve as a Backable Executive on acquisition prospecting for a Platform and/or for Bolt-On(s) for a PE leader:**

This book primarily focuses on this highly unique opportunity. This role is not that common, and most CEOs have little to no idea that many PE firms use this role to source acquisitions.

Surprisingly, roughly 80% of all PE firms have no program for using external executives for acquisition hunting.

80% of all PE firms that use an executive-first program (EFP) for sourcing acquisitions have a very weak EFP. It's not well-developed and, therefore, not phenomenally successful. It offers below-average value... so not much is done to focus on improving their program.

10% of the PE firms that do have an EFP do a good job of refining their EFP and making it a valuable tool in sourcing acquisitions.

10% of the PE firms with an EFP do a great job of highly developing their EFP, fully supporting those in the EFP, and making the EFP a very productive tool in sourcing frequent acquisitions.

Ropella 360 invests most of its valuable time in serving the 20% (cream of the crop) EFP-focused PE firms. We help them improve their EFP successfully and even upgrade select firms from good to exceptional. As you read this book, you'll learn just how we do this.

6. **Serve as a Serial Acquisition Hunter (SAH) and find multiple Platforms and then multiple Bolt-Ons as a career focus for PE firms (not always just the one PE leader):**

What's the difference between #5 and #6? Legacy wealth is achieved if you work wisely. Who do you think makes the most money in a PE firm? Seems obvious, doesn't it? It's typically the founder of the PE firm and the senior partners. Who's next on the money-earning list? Usually a Serial Acquisition Hunter. Let me explain. Like a mid-market firm in corporate America, it's the founder/CEO who makes the most, followed by the number one "hunter" business development representative.

PE firms pay very good money to source acquisition leads. As a PE firm, finding leads to acquisitions that aren't up for auction, that aren't out in the open market yet and therefore not being chased by multiple PE firms competing for the opportunity to acquire them is very hard work. Therefore, if you bring proprietary deal flow to the table on an exclusive basis to a PE firm, you can earn substantial success fees for doing so. These performance-based fees are commonly referred to as the "Lehman Formula." This commission model has been around for many years and has evolved into various alternative commission approaches, which can be very lucrative.

Also, those same PE firms will typically offer you equity in the deal beyond the performance-based acquisition fees and often will even allow you to co-invest more of your cash into the deal. This is a great way to make significant money sourcing leads, then helping with the due diligence process of making the right investments, and earning money post-acquisition through these additional investment vehicles. You can even continue to earn while supporting the scaling of the business now owned by the PE firm.

While you are serving as an acquisition hunter, you are, in a sense, creating your own PE firm because of the equity you receive and then additionally purchased. As well there is continuous cash flow for Board Seats, advising, and hunting for more acquisitions. Plus exit rewards. As acquisitions are sold, all this starts adding up to legacy wealth very quickly.

Now make a career out of being a Serial Acquisition Hunter for, say, five to 10 years... by not just chasing one acquisition and then going back to a C-Suite role, but instead staying focused on finding smaller bolt-ons, and then starting the process all over again.

For those who have this highly entrepreneurial skill set, we encourage you to AVOID the temptation to go back into a C-Suite role. Instead, take the opportunity to watch your immediate income double or triple in 1 to 2 years. Then, over the next 5 to 10 years, the possibility of increasing your legacy wealth rises by a factor of 10 to 20 times over what it might have been by going back into a C-suite role.

This is the #1 reason I authored this book – to help CEOs (or CXOs) who are interested in a path to PE wealth fully understand the massive legacy wealth opportnity of being a Serial Acquisition Hunter.

The best PE firms on the planet — those in the top 10% group (as just described above) are always looking for their next Serial Acquisition Hunter. It just so happens that these PE firms are Ropella 360's primary clients. These prestigious firms will compensate well and fully support you — most often with Ropella 360 connected as partners like a Formula 1 pit crew attached to your success. That said, Ropella 360 closely screens and only supports the best CXOs for these campaigns: those that score highly as Acquisition Hunters and, more importantly, those that choose to commit time, talent and treasure to become one.

Below is a compiled list of the 7 traits that PE Firms (and Ropella 360) look for in executives that they may back. As we get further into this book, we will also show you the Backable Executive/Acquisition Hunter Scorecard that we use on behalf of our PE clients to help them assess the absolute best executives (against the Serial Acquisition Hunter), one from the next.

The Ideal Backable Executive "Serial Hunter"

Trait 1: Former Founder/CEO with successful track record of P&L management in line with fund investment criteria.

Trait 2: Experience running a PE backed platform with a successful exit. And/or a history of M&A experience, as a buyer.

Trait 3: Has "Industry Gravitas." Is an enthusiastic subject matter expert with 15+ years of combined single Industry Sector and Market Niche recognition.

Trait 4: Understands the goal of the acquisition – to find opportunities where significant differentiation can be created, so significant growth of the acquisition can be realized.

Trait 5: Has a deep industry rolodex and insights into where Platforms and Bolt-Ons may exist.

Trait 6: Has a High IQ & EQ, is polished, persuasive, and an energetic communicator who can effectively sell his/her vision... and would be respected as a Founder/CEO coach.

Trait 7: Has initiative and is capable of commiting 6-12 months to source and close high value acquisitions.

After you've determined you have the above traits, and have scored highly on each trait, it's important you understand how Ropella 360 would partner with you. The two sections below outline what you will be responsible for and what we will be responsible for.

The Backable Executive will:

- Jointly establish a funding search strategy and campaign focus.
- Commit to transparent and precise expectation alignment regarding participation and time commitments.
- Enthusiastically pursue all generated conversations (even an exhibition match) to find the right investment partners, where all parties are excited about and willing to commit to a joint investment.
- Frequently and fully disclose Deal Flow Accelerators to ensure the firm has all the necessary information to guide and support conversations with all parties.

Ropella 360 will:

- Partner with the backable executive to develop a go-to-market strategy, focusing on targeting the right PE firms to make introductions on behalf of the backable executive.
- Develop a joint go-to-market strategy that allows backable executives to introduce themselves to targeted and actionable PE firms.
- Partner with backable executive to create a Thesis Presentation for exploratory discussions with PE firms.
- Use Ropella's business development plan to create red-carpet introductions to prospective PE firms.
- Jointly organize follow-up execution plans and conversations.

Clear Investment Thesis + Backable Executive = Great Investment Results

7. **Serve as a Board Member over a PE firm's corporate holding(s):**

There are various ways to find board member opportunities. You can contact your peers and let them know you're available. You can promote on LinkedIn that you're looking for board seats. You can look for executive search firms or board seat networking sites and share your interests to see if they can help you connect with the right opportunities. In this case, look for firms that focus on your industry sector, and you'll get better results networking through them.

You can also target PE firms directly. Again, it is best to start looking for firms with holdings where your industry experience closely aligns with them.

Ropella 360 frequently places board members with PE firms. We actively market high-profile executives related to the PE firms we focus on serving. Using a retained search model, we recruit directly for PE firms' board members. In most cases, we are searching for executives who fit a specific skill set that our PE clients target on behalf of their holdings.

We often put executives before PE firms for other permanent hire opportunities in a billable hour consulting role and/or in an acquisition hunter role. Once this relationship is established, we've found that within a short period, the executive is routinely offered a board seat with the same PE firm we introduced them to... and is now serving as a board member over one or more of the PE firm's holdings.

8. Serve as a part-time Executive Chairman over a PE firm's corporate holding(s):

Similar to #7, this role typically evolves from an introduction to a PE firm for one of the other roles. This role is generally reserved for the most seasoned CEOs who are deemed wise, have proven highly successful, and have developed a trusted relationship with the PE firm. An Executive Chairman is strictly an advisor to the CEOs of the PE Firm's holdings.

An Executive Chairman functions like a CEO Coach, typically providing pre-scheduled, hour-long meetings every other week to determine how the CEO is doing. They may ask questions like: What's keeping you up at night with business and/or your personal life? Are you exercising and eating healthily? How are you managing work-life balance? Are you enjoying your role? Do you get the support you need from the PE firm? Have you solved the problems/issues from our previous discussions yet? If not, how are you planning to solve these problems/issues? What help do you need, and where could you go to get that help to resolve these issues faster? What's the time or goal line you have set for resolving these issues?

The CEO Coach's role is to listen and guide — not take over or solve the issues directly. They advise and stay in touch to confirm progress; better yet, that a full resolution has been made. The CEO Coach's role is setting Accountability, driving Communications, and growing Trust. The coach is a powerful tool for the CEO, and the PE firm that supports the CEO. Unsurprisingly, it tends to be an equally satisfying role for the CEO Coach. CEOs working for PE firms are under significan't pressure to move quickly and solve problems effectively, with no delays or excuses. Great CEOs are hard to find and expensive to replace. Like caring for thoroughbreds, PE firms want to know that their CEOs are healthy, happy, and highly productive. CEO Coaches help confirm to the PE Leadership that this is the case for each CEO they have over their holdings.

9. **Become a full-time employee of a PE firm as an Operating Advisor in support of a PE firm's corporate holding(s):**

These roles often originate from a relationship that evolves with a PE firm where a River Guide, Due Diligence/SME, or an Acquisition Hunter determines he or she would instead work full-time on a salary with a PE firm. The Operating Advisor role is much more involved in the day-to-day business of the PE firm's holdings than a CEO Coach.

This person might visit the holdings headquarters, plants, sales offices, and innovation centers once or twice a month and even more frequently if a crisis occurs. Instead of overseeing the CEO's status, this role is much more hands-on. It directly supports the CEO and even his senior leadership team, not just identifying issues but stepping in to help accelerate resolutions.

10. **Become a full-time Principal/VP/Fundraiser or Partner within a PE firm:**

Often, these roles are filled through three sources, which typically fall into three experience levels.

Analysts often come from top-tier MBA programs. VPs or Principals are typically promoted internally or directly recruited from other PE firms. Fundraisers in the larger PE firms usually come from high-profile consulting firms, climb the ranks of large investment banking firms, and are recruited from other large PE firms.

The highest-level leaders in PE firms are often peers of the firm's founder or very senior people the founder has recruited from his direct network to join the firm at the highest level. The best of the best are promoted to partners from within the ranks below based on their excellent critical thinking, drive, and communication skills.

11. **Become an independent Business Development Acquisition "Lead Generator" for a list of PE and other investment firms:**

This role is very much like roles 5 and 6, with one major distinction: instead of working on behalf of one PE firm, this person identifies proprietary lead flow independently, with no direct attachment to any one PE firm.

Once leads surface through their own Business Development activities, this person then shares those leads with between one and three PE firms at a time, offering each of them the opportunity on a limited-time basis to consider the merits of this acquisition prospect.

If any of the firms or all of them pass on the opportunity — he or she moves on to the next group of three. This is a straight contingency, highly entrepreneurial approach — but if that's how you're wired, it's a viable and lucrative option. Often, this can be the learning path, then on-ramp, which leads to starting your own PE firm.

12. Serve in an administrative role (over HR, Accounting, Marketing, Finance, IT, etc.) in a PE firm:

This is self-explanatory, as all PE firms need help with these services. The smallest firms outsource these requirements. The largest firms have a team of SMEs over each department, like a Fortune 500 company.

13. Start your own PE (VC or FO) firm:

Ok, now you're thinking big. There's another entire book to cover this topic. If you are seriously considering this, give me a call. I have friends who have done exactly this and would love to serve as your coach and help guide you to success. Of course, I look forward to connecting Ropella 360 to your wagon and sharing in your success.

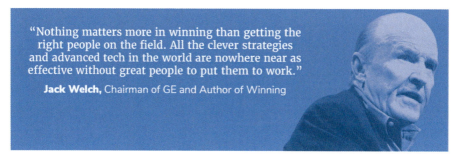

"Nothing matters more in winning than getting the right people on the field. All the clever strategies and advanced tech in the world are nowhere near as effective without great people to put them to work."

Jack Welch, Chairman of GE and Author of Winning

Chapter Three: How To Get Access to Leadership at a PE Firm

The best way to access PE firm leadership is to convince them you have something they don't have. It needs to be something of great value that can save them time and help them avoid mistakes. It seems obvious, but it's nowhere near as easy to convince them as you might think.

PE leadership is a unique breed. They are very bright, highly educated, and surrounded by other very bright and highly educated resources. Often, they believe they know everything they need to know and don't care to be proven wrong.

They are also an impatient crowd. They realize, better than anyone, that time is their greatest resource, so they are extremely cautious about not wasting it.

For these reasons, getting access to them can be highly challenging. If you don't make a good impression in the first 30 seconds you'll get cut off, and the door will likely be tough to reopen.

Of course, this may all sound like a stereotype, and — to a point — it is, but it's not entirely off base. The bottom line is this: if you reach out to PE leadership, you must be very well prepared! You've got to be highly organized in what you say to them and what you show them.

You must be able to get to the point fast. You have to convince them that you have the skills and expertise in a highly specific industry lane and, even more valuable, within a specific market niche that they already are (or should be) interested in investing in.

If you're famous in your industry, have authored a book or published articles, served as an expert witness, have been a frequent trade show or association keynote speaker, are well connected within your industry to other founders and CEOs, and are a highly accomplished business leader, then, no question, you are a world-class SME.

The leaders of PE firms are world-class investors. And good news, you both need each other.

PE firms love learning from SMEs, whom they can see as "the godfathers with gravitas" in their industry. They actively look for recognized SMEs with significant "commercial chops" — especially those still full of energy.

If the above describes you, you've got what they want: valuable information and valuable contacts or the ability to get to them surround the target acquisitions they want access to.

The primary point of "information and access" is to create deal flow. This is what PE leadership values the most; this is what they want the most. PE leaders readily admit sourcing proprietary deal flow (exclusive to them) is the hardest part of being in PE.

Your ability to guide them to the right doors and open them to founders, CEOs and/or board members (at the specific target companies within the industry and market niche that the PE firm wants to make acquisitions in) ... **is pure GOLD**.

It's also true that PE firms typically utilize three primary tools to source deal flow:

Referral Networking

Referral networking through existing portfolio/holding company relationships and executive networking generates a steady flow of possibilities. Deal flow leads can come from other private equity firms, consultants, executives, lawyers, accountants, etc. Concurrently, internal and/or external business development teams do email marketing and phone calling to surface leads. The Backable Executives campaigns described throughout this book are also an extremely valuable part of deal flow sourcing.

Deal Sourcing Platforms

There is a large and ever-changing list of Deal Sourcing Platforms that license their data and provide PE firms with access to information about companies that are on the market or maybe soon. To find them, use an internet search and/or speak with your PE sponsor who can tell you their favorites.

Investment Banking (IB) Firms

Investment bankers function much like realtors. In the PE world, most companies are bought and sold with the services of an IB. The IB collaborates with the company's leadership to help them prepare for sale, creates marketing materials, runs the sale process, conducts management meetings, provides controlled access to company leaders, manages the bidding and often the rebidding process, and controls the flow of information required to complete the due diligence process.

Sometimes, they will even help raise debt that may be required to help the buyers purchase the company. Often the IB can be hired by buyers and sellers to help with the overall negotiations of a sale or purchase.

This book focuses heavily on the power of Referral Networking:

If done right, Referral Networking is one of the most powerful ways to find proprietary deal flow.

With this in mind, Ropella 360 developed our proprietary **Deal Flow Accelerators** system, described as a two-stage, 12-step process. Like Six Sigma for Company Search, it is designed to drive both a very high-quality process **and speed**!

This is accomplished by dramatically improving the Executive First model's effectiveness, which we call **Backable Executive Campaigns**.

These are the common names used by PE for referral networking programs:

- Executive First Model
- Executive Partner Program
- Executive In Residence
- Backable Executives

There are, of course, best practices that apply to making a Backable Executive Campaign highly effective.

Over the past several years, Ropella 360 has interacted with more than 2,000 PE firms. We've carefully studied each of these PE firm's websites to determine who is marketing these programs effectively. We've also interacted with the key leadership of these firms and interviewed them about how they describe success and what percentage of success they are having with their executive first program.

We are also proud to report that we have supported more than 200 PE firms with some guidance on how they can improve their version by utilizing our Backable Executive Campaigns.

Why call it a "campaign" instead of a program or model? Like a political campaign, it must have a beginning and an end... with a clear timeline to drive urgency.

To borrow from the Formula 1 comparison, this urgency also powers the engine we call focus — the focus that drives every activity we strategize and execute. In this case, #1 alignment of expectations, #2 alignment of strategy, then #3 tactical execution. These are the 3 major parts of what drives our Deal Flow Accelerators' success, and it can be your success too.

Ropella 360 is focused on helping each client that retains us create an upgraded version (of their own) or implement the version we've created of a Backable Executive Campaign.

Utilizing the research and learnings we've accumulated from hundreds of PE firms and from the hundreds of executives we've interviewed who have participated in "Executive First Programs," we've learned a great deal about best practices.

The many executives we've interviewed tell us from their perspective what's working well for them and what's not working well — and where there's room for improvement at the PE firms with which they have partnered.

As a PE firm leader, while you are working your own Referral Networking efforts, the idea of utilizing a Backable Executive Campaign will inevitably come across your radar. How to drive success using this program will be an important question you and your team will ask. Talk to us — we can surely help!

The first thing to understand and appreciate is that:

There are three levels of Acquisition Experts

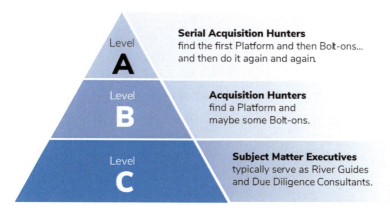

The second thing to address is:

How do we improve our own Backable Executive Campaigns?

Inside this key question, there is a set of core issues:

- How do we avoid wasting time running this kind of networking program?
- What questions do we ask to confirm that this executive is passionate about their own well-articulated thesis?
- Are they conflict-free?
- Do they have the necessary bandwidth for the timeline required?
- Will they stay loyal to our campaign?
- Will they stay focused all the way through the finish line?
- Will they achieve ultimate success and acquire a platform?
- And then, in an ideal world, carry forward that success by sourcing needed bolt-ons?
- How do we use/improve the Backable Executive Campaign to maximize success while sourcing highly focused proprietary deal flow?

The way to increase the likelihood of success is all about effective partnering.

Whether you are selling your company to a PE firm, are planning to be a Backable Executive in partnership with a PE firm, or you're part of running a PE firm, it's extremely important that you all think equally and intensely about the requirement of aligning interests in accordance with the charter of the fund and the goals of the limited partners.

That's the key to getting the interest, approval, support, and decision-making required to make the partnership successful.

The PE firm defines the first level of success as closed acquisitions. The second level of success is scaling the business and making it profitable.

When all parties are investing their time, talent, and treasure and are highly aligned around fit, the odds of success on both levels are dramatically increased. Having skin in the game matters, but the Right Fit matters more!

Executives Partnering with PE successfully... is all about the:

Right PE Experience Fit
(exp. running PE Platforms, with a successful exit & M&A Exp from the Buy Side)

Right Industry Expertise Fit
(SME expertise in the Chemical Industry with a Deep Rolodex and Valuable Insights)

Right Thesis Focus Fit
(SME expertise in Chemical based Food Ingredients)

Right Personality Fit
(CEO EQ, Sales Ability & CEO Coaching skills, all with Passion)

Right Motivation
(Time = 3-6-12 months, Talent & Treasure = Cash + Sweat Equity + Network of Resources)

Right Due Diligence Support Services & Resources Fit
(Trained Bus Dev Hunters as Cold Calling Team & an available, Responsive PE Partner)

Character, Competence, and Cost
(Cost = Your Time, Talent, and Treasure)
are what get you through the door.

Accountability, Communications, and Trust.
How you ACT is what keeps you at the table.

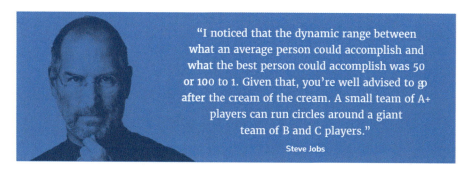

"I noticed that the dynamic range between what an average person could accomplish and what the best person could accomplish was 50 or 100 to 1. Given that, you're well advised to go after the cream of the cream. A small team of A+ players can run circles around a giant team of B and C players."

Steve Jobs

PART TWO
FINDING THE RIGHT PE PARTNER

Chapter Four: Screening The Right PE Firms to Consider Working With

The Right Executive

The most successful PE firms take extreme care in selecting the right Backable Executive for a thesis-driven "buy & build" campaign. The right executive will be required to uniquely balance several activities while displaying traits fundamental to driving success through a "Backable Executive Campaign."

When retained by our clients, Ropella 360 focuses on the Seven Traits of Backable Executives outlined in Chapter 2 to effectively screen and score the Backable Executive prospects.

Beyond reviewing a LinkedIn page and resume, we then conduct a half-hour or more phone interview with each candidate we are considering, ensuring we uncover exactly how good a fit each candidate may be.

We then collect a deep dive Skills Survey from every candidate to analyze how serious they are and how strong a fit they may be while working as a Backable Executive with our PE client. We organize all the data we evaluate on a perspective candidate using a Scorecard to help us decide whom we may select for submission to our PE clients.

At Ropella 360, we take this very seriously and invest significant time focusing on "the right fit" for our PE client with every Backable Executive we submit. As a Backable Executive, you should also carefully collect data on each PE firm you are considering and the people you will be interacting and partnering with. Think carefully through this important decision as you prepare to select the right PE firm fit.

A sample of our generic Skills Survey and Scorecard is on the next two pages. These items are customized when a client retains us. In this case, we conduct a Search Preparation Conference Call with the PE firm leadership team and determine alignment around key "Must Haves" that support the rough draft investment thesis. Then, we compile custom questions around those specifics. Once the Skills Survey is complete, we will modify the Scorecard layout to match the Skills Survey.

These two tools were developed as part of The SMART Search System, which we created more than 20 years ago while growing our executive search business. We like to describe this system as akin to "Six Sigma for Executive Search." It's all about collecting more data earlier in the interview process so we ask better questions early on and drive better decision-making.

Skill Survey — **The DEAL FLOW Accelerator System** — Powered By Ropella360

Executive
Title **Backable Executive**

1. In which specific industry niches do you consider yourself a "Subject Matter Expert"? Which of these are you especially credible in and (equally important) most passionate about?

2. If you had to pick just one lane that you have the most experience in and/or are most passionate about - how would you answer this question - Where do you see opportunity and excitement in this specific thesis lane?

3. Briefly outline the level of full P&L responsibility ($) you have held in current or past C-Suite positions.

4. Do you have prior experience serving as an executive in a Private Equity-backed company? If so, did this result in or lead to an exit? Please include an estimate of the return generated to investors and the revenue/EBITDA at the time of purchase and/or sale.

5. Describe any merger and acquisition activities you have been personally responsible for negotiating and closing? What was the most challenging part of post-acquisition integration and which strategies/tools have you found most valuable to enable a successful transition?

6. Are you interested in making a meaningful co-investment alongside the right PE Firm with the potential of dedicating up to 12 months to a company search project?

7. Have you ever taken a personal proactive approach to sourcing acquisition prospects? What is your willingness to make "Gold Calls" to a shortlist of prospects and/or take the lead for high priority targets that are identified?

8. At what level(s) would you be interested in and able to dedicate your time in a partnership with Private Equity? Directly supporting the successful sourcing and closing of an acquisition and then…

    a) transitioning to a full-time C-Suite executive role within that organization.

    b) working for the PE firm as an Operating Partner; a "One-and-Done Acquisition Hunter."

    c) repeatedly seeking out additional platforms/bolt-ons; a "Serial Acquisition Hunter."

    Otherwise, interested in alternative roles serving as an SME due diligence advisor, as a full-time/interim CEO, and/or as a board member.

Ropella360.com | Skill Survey

The Right PE Firm

Now that you know more about PE firms and how they work, it's time to start looking more closely at how each firm operates when considering the right PE firm fit for you. As you work through the process of partnering with a PE firm, you will experience the typical Buy & Build PE strategy and will be asked to be involved in the race to complete a platform acquisition, then asked to find and acquire bolt-ons, and then likely asked to assist (as a leadership team executive, Board member, or acquisition hunter) towards generating a successful exit.

> Backable Executive Scorecard

Ropella 360
A catalyst for connection

Interviewer's Name: _____   Date: _____

Candidate's Name: _____   Position: _____

1. Experience at C-Suite for at least 3 years (CEO, CFO, COO, or equivalent).
   Notes/Details:
   ☐ Yes ☐ No
   Score: 1-3

2. Primary P&L responsibility with companies sized:
   Notes/Details:
   Low ($5M - $50M Rev.) ☐
   Middle ($50M - $500M Rev.) ☐
   High ($500M+ Revenue) ☐

3. Experience running a PE-backed platform with a successful exit.
   Notes/Details:
   ☐ Yes ☐ No
   Score: 1-3

4. M&A strategy involvement (deal table and/or due diligence leadership) as a buyer.
   Notes/Details:
   ☐ Yes ☐ No
   Score: 1-3

5. Has subject matter expertise, with industry gravitas, in a specific industry segment.
   Notes/Details:
   ☐ Yes ☐ No
   Score: 1-3

6. Has a deep industry rolodex of contacts with founders and CEOs of potential targets and others to leverage for sourcing.
   Notes/Details:
   ☐ Yes ☐ No
   Score: 1-3

7. Has high IQ and EQ. Polished, persuasive, effective communicator, and an energetic CEO coach.
   Notes/Details:
   ☐ Yes ☐ No
   Score: 1-3

8. Is motivated and capable of committing to a 6-12 month campaign to successfully close high value acquisitions – in partnership with Deal Flow Accelerators.
   Notes/Details:
   ☐ Yes ☐ No
   Score: 1-3

9. They possess unique insights into opportunities where significant differentiation can pave the way for 3-5X EBITDA growth.
   Notes/Details:
   ☐ Yes ☐ No
   Score: 1-3

Powered By **SMART**^{SM} Search System
Recruit smarter. Not harder.

☐ A = Acquisition Hunter
☐ B = Backable Exec / SME
☐ C = SME Alone

Total Score (8-24)
_____

> The PE Acquisition Playbook

Experienced Management Partnering with Experienced Investors

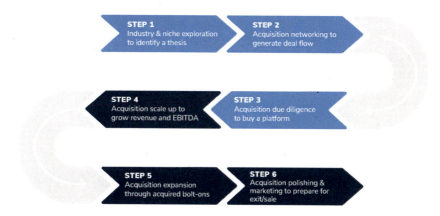

During this six-step "Buy & Build" process, there can be a lot of ups and downs. You'll experience highly enthusiastic days, and then stressful days, and even rather depressing days. Just like past career roles, the quality of your supervisors, peers, and subordinates (the team) can make all the difference between your success or failure, as well as your satisfaction or dissatisfaction during the day-to-day partnership. Therefore, when interviewing, you should consider the right PE firm fit very carefully, because that's what PE firms are trying to achieve too.

You should also have your own survey checklist to screen each PE firm you consider and a corresponding scorecard to organize and track all of your collected data.

Think of the Backable Executive role as a role that will often evolve into a long-term opportunity, like a series of "racing seasons," while partnering with a PE firm as a Serial Acquisition Hunter. Most PE firm leadership will want you to look well beyond a one-year race season, as they typically want more than a one-off race (one acquisition and done).

The PE firm's leadership team will invest substantial time, talent, and treasure to support you as their high-performance driver and develop you into a world-class Acquisition Hunter targeting a platform and then bolt-ons.

That said, the most legacy wealth comes from becoming a Serial Acquisition Hunter as you repeat this process over and over. Sure, you can make good money on a one-off acquisition and great money if you do a platform and a series of bolt-on acquisitions. But if you enjoy the experience, consider making a career out of it through closely related adjacencies to your industry expertise.

If you are reading this book as a founder or CEO focused on selling a business, this chapter is just as important to you.

As you progress in being evaluated by PE firms, you should study the PE firms' websites and other internet searches to learn as much as you can about each PE firm before you get into deep interviews with any of them.

Your long list of prospective firms might have up to 20 that fit your focus.

Your lenses used to hone in your focus should include:

The industry fit:

Between your experience/network/passions and the PE firms' current holdings or interests.

Your market niche fit:

Suppose you've worked mostly in the food industry. More specifically, mostly with ingredients that affect shelf life, and the PE firm wants you to focus on acquisitions in the auto body industry. How's this going to fit? It's an extreme example, but hyper-specific fit matters to everyone involved.

Your geographic fit:

If you're in Florida and the PE firm is in Europe and, once you're acquired, they want to see you face to face regularly, how will this fit? Or if you are tired of traveling and want to focus locally on acquisition hunting (to scale your company faster), and they want you to "go global," how will this fit?

Your size of target acquisitions fit:

If your entire career has been spent working with or serving Fortune 500 companies, and they want you to focus on targeting small business acquisitions, how will this fit?

The performance of the PE firm fit:

Using the metrics mentioned in the previous chapter — how well are the funds doing within the PE firms you are considering? Ask the questions:

What's the typical IRR for your funds?

Typical MOIC?

Are your funds typically top Quartile?

Your cultural fit:

What are your values and morals? Who are you? How will politics, religion, nationality, generational differences, and other "hot topics" affect your interactions? Now's the time to clarify everything.

Your relationship Fit:

How well do you feel you will get along and be able to respect the PE team, especially the senior leadership at the firm? What's the average tenure or turnover of employees at the three levels? Ask if there are references you can speak with at those levels.

Your control fit:

How "hands-on vs. hands-off" does this feel? What is their approach to managing people like you, and are you comfortable with that approach? What's their governance philosophy for their holdings? How often do they make CEO changes among most of their acquisitions?

Your support fit:

If you're a CEO who's used to large support teams, and they don't have them, how is this going to fit?

Your exclusivity fit:

If they are open to you serving on other boards, on other consulting projects, or even assisting other firms vs. NOT — how's this going to fit?

What is your take on their experience with Executive First/Backable Executive campaigns?

Is this a test project, or are they well-practiced utilizing this approach? Ask them, "what's been your typical results when doing acquisition hunting or partnering with people like me?"

Then, finally, how are you going to be compensated during:

- the acquisition hunting process,
- at the close of an acquisition, and,
- at the sale of an acquisition (where you specifically helped the PE firm source the acquisition)?

Chapter Five: Scoring The Right PE Firms With Which You're Interviewing

The lenses in Chapter 4 all seem obvious, don't they? I think we can all agree on that point. That being said, the bigger issue is how you get the answers to these questions and then track those answers to make a more logical decision. You do that with a Scorecard tailored around the right PE partner for your situation.

Collect your data, then start scoring each answer with a Low, Middle, or High score. When the Scorecard is completed, give a low score a 1, a middle score a 2, and a high score a 3. You can even use bonus points for what matters to you more. Then, add up the points and see how each firm compares.

Like due diligence when considering an acquisition, smart decisions are all about gathering data. The more data you can uncover and consider before conducting interviews makes for smarter go or no-go decisions... and better final decisions.

Now that you have your own Scorecard set up and you've incorporated data from your preliminary review, the next step is to set up phone conversations with your preferred PE targets to narrow down that list of screened firms.

Ultimately, you will want to set up "Fireside Chats" with the top three to five finalist firms that you've narrowed down from your long list. Remember, continue to update your scorecards (one for each PE Firm) as you move through each successive step.

As a Backable Executive, you shouldn't make your selection based on who will offer the most money upfront. You need to consider this like an entrepreneurial venture. Which partnering opportunity makes the most financial sense from the beginning to the end?

Upfront money is nice, but the more you accept at the start, the less risk you take and the fewer rewards you typically will get on the back end. It's better to focus on where and with whom you're going to maximize the greatest odds of having significant success as an Acquisition Hunter and then ultimately as a Serial Acquisition Hunter. Often, these career transitions are three-to-seven-year stints, so play the long game and watch your investment portfolio explode with value.

If you're looking for PE firms as a potential seller and just want to retire and walk away — the best price offer can make the most sense. But, if you want to stay engaged as a chairman, board member, or advisor, you should seriously consider rolling equity forward in the deal. Especially so if and you care about how this sale will affect your key leadership team and your employees at large who stay post-acquisition.

Therefore there's more to it than just upfront money. Picking the right firm matters greatly, because it's how the relationship is managed after the sale that determines the ultimate value.

Successful Backable Executive Campaigns all boil down to this; The Right Executive with the Right Thesis and the Right Support moves the needle with greater quality and then speed.

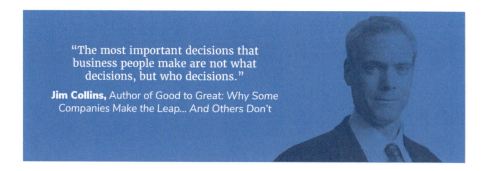

"The most important decisions that business people make are not what decisions, but who decisions."

Jim Collins, Author of Good to Great: Why Some Companies Make the Leap... And Others Don't

PART THREE

DEVELOPING THE PE PARTNERSHIP STRATEGY

Chapter Six: Before You Start Racing with PE, Develop a Winning Strategy

The development of the Backable Executive Campaign is based on more than 1,000 survey responses and 200 interviews with PE firms and Backable Executives from the lower and middle markets.

Ropella 360 has learned that while most firms seek to differentiate their business development efforts, few commit the time and effort required to realize significant differentiation and success with their own Executive First programs.

To combat this challenge, Ropella 360 has developed an interactive workbook to help firms develop a clear path to obtaining scalable ROI through our recently launched Deal Flow Accelerator program. The next section of this book will focus on how we help CEOs and their PE sponsor move together, smarter, with greater quality and speed. Just like a Formula 1 race team! Zoom!

For years, The Ropella Group had provided three different service offerings to make the above happen. In 2023, we determined it was time for a rebrand... and Ropella 360 was the result. Through extensive branding and marketing research and www.ropella360.com was proudly launched in January 2024.

We determined that we needed to combine the three different firms that we had created over the previous years: 1) Ropella Executive Search, 2) Ropella Equity Ventures (our PE Services Firm), and 3) Xcavate, an Information Research Firm, into one firm, with one website, thereby providing a clearer and more cohesive branding message.

So, the new combined Ropella 360 home page states:

Ropella 360 serves as Strategic Advisors to PE Firms, Middle Market firms, and Fortune 500 clients from across the globe.

Providing People for Executive Search and Platform Search and Perspectives Search while helping grow your great company faster.

We do so through strategically considered industry/market/product specific introductions to A-players and Level 5, Transformational C-Suite Leaders and SME Advisors.

For those requiring the highest levels of value creation, working with Ropella 360 means leveraging the world's best leaders and uncovering untapped growth opportunities and proprietary M&A deals to drive more significant investor ROI.

Throughout the first half of this book, we've focused heavily on finding the right fit between the people (the industry executives and the PE Firm leadership). We've also focused on how PE firms identify the right platforms that fit their investment goals.

Now, we will dive deep into how they develop strategic plans to target individual acquisitions within the thesis lane in which they are interested in investing. Perspectives form the foundational information that keeps everyone focused like a laser beam on reaching the right targets.

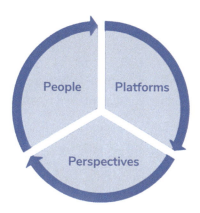

The Right Thesis – supported by the Right Perspectives

There are two common approaches to developing and implementing investment theses regarding thesis development:

1. Starting with an executive with a thesis, or
2. The PE firm producing a thesis and then sourcing an executive to execute it.

Each approach has its own set of pros and cons. Here is a brief outline of the pros and cons of each approach:

Executive First, Then Thesis:

Pros:

- Deep Expertise: The executive typically has deep industry knowledge and experience, which can lead to a more insightful and realistic thesis.
- Commitment and Vision: An executive with a personal thesis may be more committed and enthusiastic about its success.
- Rapid Execution: The executive can hit the ground running, leveraging their expertise and network from day one.

Cons:

- Limited Scope: The thesis might be limited to the executive's area of expertise, potentially missing broader market opportunities.
- Risk of Bias: The executive's personal biases and past experiences could skew the thesis, potentially overlooking certain risks or alternative strategies.
- Challenge in Finding the Right Match: Finding an executive with the right thesis and skills can be time-consuming and often challenging for the PE firm.

PE Firm Develops Thesis, Then Finds Executive:

Pros:

- Broader Perspective: The PE firm can develop a thesis based on wide-ranging market research and insights, potentially identifying more diverse opportunities.
- Risk Mitigation: The PE firm can build a thesis that considers a range of factors and scenarios, which might better mitigate risks.

- Flexibility in Execution: The firm can source an executive whose skills and experience perfectly fit the specific thesis.

Cons:

- Time to Implementation: Finding the right executive to execute the thesis typically takes a lot of time, delaying the investment process.
- Lack of Immediate Expertise: The sourced executive might need time to fully understand and adapt to the thesis, especially if it's outside their prior focused experience.
- Possible Lack of Commitment: An executive brought in after the thesis is developed may not be as personally invested in the idea as someone who created it themselves.

For these reasons, Ropella 360 strongly suggests integrating thesis development with executive identification. In other words, bringing the right executive in at the very front end of the process is best.

In the Executive First model, the PE firm starts by outlining a preliminary investment thesis based on broad market research and initial insights. Often, SME advisors narrow down the broad industry sector(s) to a more focused "river" or product/market niche segment. Then, the PE firm utilizes a River Guide to better understand this specific investment path.

The River Guide and PE firm's strategy team then develop a draft thesis. Typically, the thesis is not fully fleshed out yet, but it serves as a solid foundation for continued discussion. The firm then decides it is time to actively seek executives who align with this preliminary thesis and bring their deep industry expertise and innovative perspectives to the next step: the acquisition-hunting phase.

During the Backable Executive search process, the thesis is collaboratively refined, combining the firm's market understanding with the executive's specialized knowledge and vision. This approach fosters a strong sense of ownership and commitment from the executive as they shape the thesis from an early stage. Simultaneously, it ensures that the investment strategy benefits from the broader market perspective and risk assessment capabilities of the PE firm.

The end result is a more robust and dynamic investment thesis tailored to leverage the executive's strengths and insights and backed by the PE firm's strategic and analytical resources.

In support of this uniquely balanced approach, Ropella 360 proposes using a

Backable Executive/Thesis Scorecard alongside a tiered hierarchy of focus to guide meaningful and productive executive selection and collaboration. More on that in the next chapter. Read on.

It's time to get laser-focused on where the PE Firm and its Backable Executive will focus, where they will target acquisition prospects, and how they will do so.

The keener the focus, the greater the results and the faster they come. We have invested 35 years conducting searches for every type of high-tech company you can imagine, from chemicals to biotech, nanotech to 3D printing, fighter jet electronics to nuclear power, battery-powered cars, and more! Often, our searches are for people with extremely particular skill sets and we search all over the globe. We describe ourselves as "needle in haystack" search experts with a 95% success rate.

We've learned search is search is search! Whether you are searching for people, or searching for perspectives/information, or searching for companies to acquire, it's all about process, systemization, and a relentless pursuit of FOCUS. Here's how the best PE firms look at the importance of focus:

The Hierarchy of Focus for a Backable Executive "Acquisition Hunter"

Level A Focus
Targeting the same EXIT that the CEO (now Aquisition Hunter) just experienced. Same Industry & Market focus. Same Mfg/Products & Niche Applications. Let's use what we already know and duplicate the same success. **Find a Platform, then find Bolt-ons.**

Level B Focus
Targeting closely affiliated areas the CEO crossed over or into. Could be customers or indirect competitors closely connected to the targets described above. Let's use what we know to get answers to where we have gaps. **Find a Platform, then find Bolt-ons.**

Level C Focus
Targeting related Industry segments where business / manufacturing processes and customer services are very similar to the CEOs expertise. **Find a Platform, then find Bolt-ons.**

Once you have sorted out the focus that the PE firm and the Backable Executive will have as part of their partnership, it's time to test the validity of the focused thesis by scoring the thesis on how well-developed it is when compared to the person(s) who is/are going to be responsible for executing it.

Obviously, the higher the score, the more likely success will be and the more likely it is to drive quality interactions with prospective company sellers faster.

After extensive research and much practice, this is the Ropella 360 Thesis Scorecard we use.

The Thesis Scorecard

Trait 1 — How well does this thesis line up with the backable CEO's specific industry subject matter expertise and experience?

Trait 2 — How well does this thesis line up as it relates to acquisition target size and with the company size experience of the backable CEO's?

Trait 3 — How well developed is this thesis as of right now?
Low = only in simplistic draft form
Middle = relatively well thought out and laid out on paper
High = well thought and well documented

Trait 4 — Does the Thesis Creator have money to invest or a network of potential investors?

Trait 5 — How well does the thesis (lane, topic) line up with the PE firm's investment interest? For Example: $5M to $40M EBITDA, Enterp. Value of $500M, Equity Invest. of $50 to $250M

Trait 6 — In this industry segment, are there opportunities where significant differentiation can be created so considerable growth of the acquisition can be realized? For example: tech, products, brands, markets, mfg., geographies, etc.

Trait 7 — Are there targets in play?
A) Identified & Contacted
B) Identified but not contacted
C) No clear targets identified yet

Trait 8 — Do we have a tangible and compelling strategy and call to action that will resonate with owner entrepreneurs?

Trait 9 — Do we understand what the future buyers value to drive an above average multiple?

Once a Backable Executive has determined their ideal thesis, and decided they want to partner with a PE firm, and we have determined they are a good fit for our program, the below is an overview of how we would package them for submission to our PE client. This is what we call a **Backable Executive Thesis Report**.

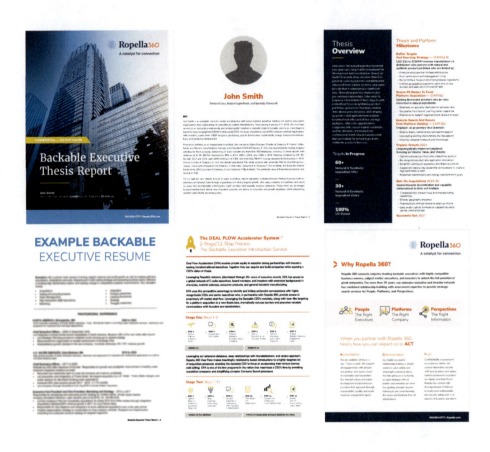

Sometimes the executive has a clear thesis that's well articulated. They bring most of the content to the table, and we simply polish it into a tight presentation for submission to the PE firm.

In other cases, we work with a PE firm on the thesis and build it out into a presentation with the PE firm. Then we find a Backable Executive who is extremely qualified to represent the thesis and passionate about it as well. We then tweak the content around the executive that the PE firm brought forward.

If you have a thesis in mind, please reach out to us, and we'll discuss how we can partner with you to help your vision become a successful reality faster.

Chapter Seven: Executing Your PE Race Strategy With Goals and Timetables

The RIGHT Fit with your PE Sponsor is extremely important as a review. Carefully consider: **is the particular PE firm you're about to engage with the right fit for you?**

Below is an example of how we look at the Right Fit. This example is based on a chemical industry executive with specific experience in the food ingredients space.

CEO's Partnering with PE successfully... is all about the:

Right PE Experience Fit
(exp. running PE Platforms, with a successful exit & M&A Exp from the Buy Side)

Right Industry Expertise Fit
(SME expertise in the Chemical Industry with a Deep Rolodex and Valuable Insights)

Right Thesis Focus Fit
(SME expertise in Chemical based Food Ingredients)

Right Personality Fit
(CEO EQ, Sales Ability & CEO Coaching skills, all with Passion)

Right Motivation
(Time = 3-6-12 months, Talent & Treasure = Cash + Sweat Equity + Network of Resources)

Right Due Diligence Support Services & Resources Fit
(Trained Bus Dev Hunters as Cold Calling Team & an available, Responsive PE Partner)

Character, Competence, and Cost
(Cost = Your Time, Talent, and Treasure)
are what get you through the door.

Accountability, Communications, and Trust.
How you ACT is what keeps you at the table.

If this feels like a strong yes, then keep in mind that your primary goal for engaging with this specific PE firm is to obtain acquisition success.

Once you have successfully closed an acquisition with your PE Partners, you'll typically be asked to participate in the strategic planning for scaling up the acquisition. You'll be looking at growth strategies that typically fall into these three buckets: Organic, Margin Expansion, and Buy and Build.

The goal is to accelerate the acquired platform's growth and prepare the business for the next sale for at least 3X MOIC. Remember, this will also drive exponential growth in your investment portfolio.

While that is happening, you must be ready to roll right into phase two: hunting for viable bolt-ons. Once that's completed, you should plan to start over and repeat the process again and again. Short of owning your own PE firm, this is the fastest way to generate massive generational wealth.

With that reminder in place, let's examine how we drive the thesis focus into the first stage of thesis execution.

The following pages provide a sample of a Backable Thesis Executive Report created between a Backable Executive and his PE sponsor. Every single one of these Thesis Reports is customized around the following:

- The investment ambitions of the PE firm.
- The thesis expertise and passions that support the Acquisition Hunting role of the Backable Executive.
- The data collected, and information analysis that drive the focus of the partnership.

Again, the PE firm typically starts with an overview of related industries. Then, with the help of a River Guide, the PE firm narrows down the industries to identify one of interest. Together with the Backable Executive, they narrow the industry to a specific Product/Market Sector. This drives the thesis beyond a draft into a specific and highly focused strategic planning document.

A thesis evolved from this one-image graphic...

Thesis Evaluation & Development

Backable Executive Thesis Report

For: Bob Johnson with: ABC 123 Private Equity

Personal Care Thesis Overview

Investing in the Personal Care Value Chain is a compelling opportunity, given the scarcity of target companies resulting from significant consolidation within the middle market. This consolidation has also underscored the notable service gap for customers, highlighting the potential for enhanced customer experiences and satisfaction. With the personal care industry continuing to show steady growth and consumer demand, strategic investments in this value chain through small to medium-sized businesses offer the potential for substantial returns and market leadership.

Then the graphic evolved into this detailed presentation.

Cover slide:

Now it's time to dive deep into identifying the acquisition targets as described above.

This is where a search strategy conference call with XCAVATE begins.

www.xcavate.com

A conference call with XCAVATE leads to a Research Strategy document that outlines all the company targets worth reaching out to for relationship building. The sourcing, screening, and organization of this large list of companies and contacts leads to a targeted list to network for acquisition prospects.

Slide 1 is an example of how the Research Strategy is combined into the Backable Executive Thesis Report. This report is used by the PE Leader to steer the Acquisition Hunting Lunch Meeting — where the execution steps between the Acquisition Hunting team are mapped out.

Slide 1:

Slide summarizes the market and provides data collected through various market research sources.

Slide 2:

Executing Your Race Strategy with Goals and Timetables

Slide 3:

This is where we strategize and prioritize the target company list.

Slide 4:

This slide demonstrates a possible Platform & Bolt-ons scenario. Created simply to start dialogue around envisioning success scenarios.

Once everyone on the Acquisition Hunting team is 100% in agreement on the thesis and the focused targeting is completed for the business development team to start prospecting on, the next step is to prepare for live phone calls.

At Ropella 360 we are a Catalyst for Connection. We focus first and foremost on building solid relationship foundations on behalf of the Backable Executive and the selected PE firm, with all our connections.

We are SuperConnectors at heart. Our LinkedIn, other social media platforms, and proprietary networking database combined with licensed databases are as large as any of the most successful "Social Media Influencers," with our own followers counting in the millions.

It took us more than 35 years to build a network this large. We protect the integrity and confidentiality of the contacts in this combined network extremely carefully.

It's relationships that make a great brand. These relationships ignite while proving character, competence, and cost (cost is what you're willing to personally invest. it equals your own: time, talent and treasure).

Relationships grow through how we all ACT (Accountability, Communications, and Trust). Especially when there are challenges, pressure, and stresses that test the value of the relationship. The combination of the three Cs, ACT, and a commitment to never give up, makes valuable relationships last.

Referral Networking is the most important and most powerful form of relationship marketing for a business-to-business firm like ours. While running Backable Executive campaigns, we typically make hundreds of phone calls on behalf of the executive and their PE sponsor. The success of our referral networking (phone calling campaigns) is based on establishing and then maintaining what we describe as our **Circle of Trust**:

Often, Ropella 360 launches a relationship with a new connection by helping a PE client or a corporate technology C-suite leader with their executive search needs. We collaborate with clients and candidates and connect the right "**PEOPLE**" who are needed in senior leadership ranks within holdings, on boards, and/or within PE Firms. We also place many SME consultants.

Because of our SMART Search System, our candidates and clients alike experience satisfaction and success, learning to believe firsthand in our capabilities and creating a willingness to trust us.

Then, we help them search for a **PLATFORM** (mergers, acquisitions, JVs, and/or funding for platforms and bolt-ons). We help our candidates and clients while collecting valuable information that they've determined they need to form **PERSPECTIVES**.

By successfully providing these services at the highest quality levels, delivered very fast, we become highly valued, strategic advisors to these A-player and Level 5/Transformational Leaders, who refer us to others in their networks.

In summary, our relationships always start with **PEOPLE** (where the Circle of Trust begins), and there the foundations are laid by proving **CHARACTER**, **COMPETENCE**, and **COST**. Relationships grow deeper as we provide valuable services (through **PLATFORMS** and **PERSPECTIVES**), and ultimately, we are generating long-lasting relationships through **ACCOUNTABILITY, COMMUNICATIONS**, and **TRUST**.

The Ropella 360 Suite
Your Own Personal SuperConnector Resource... Providing SEARCH Services for:

People
The Right Executives

Identifying A-players & Level 5 transformational leaders as:

- Board members
- C-Suite executives
- Key leaders & team builders
- PE leadership
- Interim SMEs & consultant

Platforms
The Right Company

Partnering with founders, innovators, and investors on:

- Sourcing backable CEOs
- Buy-side deal flow
- Sell-side transactions
- Investment possibilities

Perspectives
The Right Information

Directing XCAVATE Search Strategy for:

- Company list building
- Executive list building
- Sell-side transactions
- List sorting and prioritizing

Now, it's time to start preparing to make phone calls to the founders, C-suite leaders, and/or board members of the prospective target companies that the PE firm is interested in potentially acquiring.

The PE firms we are selling our services to will often tell us that they have found it more effective for executives to make calls to prospective acquisition targets than for a company search firm to do so, as they have a long-standing reputation in the market and can connect with business owners on an operator-to-operator level, unlike an investor or broker.

To a point, this is true. Still, these Backable Executives haven't done cold calling for years, if ever. They are also used to having secretaries, assistants, sales, and marketing teams as supporters to do much of the execution for them. Now, the PE firm is typically expecting them to do pretty much everything themselves.

Yes, these executives will admit that they have connections, and they will make cold calls. However, we find their connections run dry, typically within a week or two, and the number of phone calls they can "connect with" is a very short list. Some do better than others, but most of these PE-led campaigns fail. From what we've learned from many PE firms and the executives who have worked on these campaigns (without a strong business development networking team supporting them), the failure rate of the PE-led campaigns is well over 80%.

Several factors drive this failure rate. We've talked at length about the right fit between the Backable Executive, the PE firm, and the target acquisition audience. The lack of the right fit is a major reason campaigns start and fizzle out after 30 days. The lack of Bcakable Executive support is also a major factor.

This is exactly what drove the development of the Deal Flow Accelerator System. While identifying the right Backable Executive and thesis are foundational to a successful "Executive First" business development approach, many PE firms struggle to commit the time and resources necessary to realize significant differentiation and success with their internal programs. Providing the right resources is like "flipping the tables" from an 80% failure rate to an 80% success rate.

This is where Ropella 360 delivers with our Deal Flow Accelerators System.

The DEAL FLOW Accelerator System[SM]
2-Stage/12-Step Process
The Backable Executive Introduction Service

Deal Flow Accelerators (DFA) enables private equity to establish strong partnerships with industry-leading transformational executives so that together they can acquire and build companies while applying a backable executive's vision or thesis.

Leveraging Ropella's network developed through 35+ years of executive search, DFA has access to a global network of C-suite executives, board members, and investors with extensive backgrounds in chemicals, material sciences, and general industrial manufacturing.

DFA uses this competitive advantage to identify and initiate actionable conversations with highly recognizable Executives. Who, in partnership with Ropella 360, provide access to proprietary off-market deal flow. Leveraging the backable executive's notoriety, along with laser-like targeting for a platform acquisition in a new thesis lane, dramatically reduces barriers and promotes valuable conversations with founders and stakeholders.

Stage One — Steps 1-6

- STEP 1: Explore Platform or Bolt-on Thesis
- STEP 2: Discuss Ideal Profiles and Acquisition Targets
- STEP 3: Prepare Backable Executive Search Collateral
- STEP 4: Review Executive Profiles
- STEP 5: Conduct Interviews and Confirm Thesis Fit
- STEP 6: Finalize Backable Executive's Engagement Letter

WEEKS 1-3 | WEEKS 3-12

Leveraging our extensive database, deep relationships with founder/owners, and unique approach, Ropella 360 makes meaningful introductions to a highly-targeted list of acquisition prospects, enabling the backable executive to focus on accelerating their venture.

DFA is one of the few programs in the nation that maximizes an executive's time by providing acquisition prospects and simplifying complex processes.

Stage Two — Steps 7-12

STEP 7 Confirm Platform or Bolt-On Acquisition Target List

STEP 8 Begin Deal Flow Networking Campaign

STEP 9 Conduct Exploratory Discussions With Owners

STEP 10 Term Sheet/LOI Submissions

STEP 11 Conduct Due Diligence and Close Platform Deal

STEP 12 Identify Add-On Acquisition and Begin Step 9 Again

WEEK 12 TO 6 MONTHS | TYPICALLY COMPLETED WITHIN 6 MONTHS TO 1 YEAR

So, beyond what's outlined above, how does Deal Flow Accelerators work? The secret sauce is special. It's about building a team of very sharp cold calling "Hunters." All confident, competitive athletes and sharp minds who love talking and are highly polished communicators — just what PE firms like to hire.

In addition to these traits, they are extremely well-trained sales professionals screened as hunters, NOT farmers. There's a huge difference between hunters and farmers. Hunters are wired by God to have the right curiosity, drive, and never-give-up attitude. Only one in 20 practicing salespeople fit this hunter profile, and it's a primary focus in our hiring. Sounds straightforward and easy, right?

No way! This has been the most difficult challenge of my 40-year sales, sales management, and entrepreneurial career. Building this team of lions is like operating as a lion tamer in a three-ring circus. I frequently joke that they'll eat me if I don't keep them happy, under control, and well-fed.

We design every campaign so that calls are maximized, voicemail messages are returned, and texts/emails receive a reply. We support this team with world-class processes and procedures for everything they do.

They get the best computers, software, licenses, and office space. We support them with continuous training, information research, database management, and marketing. We describe our Business Development team as a Formula 1 race team... and it's no joke. We love to win, and we hate to lose.

The likelihood of our success in delivering an expedited, high-quality experience to our client (the PE firm and Backable Executive combined) is predicated heavily on this team. We are scaling this team and refining everything we do as we strive to win every race.

If this interests you, please reach out to us to learn more at **ropella360.com**.

Chapter Eight: Compensation and Incentivization While Creating Generational Wealth

Now that you've selected the PE firm that best suits you and the PE firm says it wants to be your sponsor, it's time to begin crafting a partnership agreement.

This agreement must be a win–win for everyone involved. It should motivate you, be designed to keep you attached to a certain timeline and a high-level of exclusivity, and drive a certain level of "intrapreneurial" risk for the rewards received.

We know this is what the Backable Executive wants. It just so happens that most PE firms also want this in their Backable Executive.

Now, it's about keeping the balance of give and take and the emotions in check as the negotiations are completed, so at the "closing," everyone is satisfied there's a win-win agreement being approved that will last.

So, you might ask, how can a PE leader best incentivize and motivate a Backable Executive to improve the odds of Deal Flow success?

While Backable Executive compensation programs vary widely across the lower, middle, and upper-middle market segments, Ropella 360 has found that the most successful firms utilize a matrix of compensation mechanisms to ensure alignment and retention from the beginning to the end of a thesis-led buy-and-build strategy.

Before we get into the details, it's important to recognize that the size of a PE firm will likely dictate the flexibility of the budget for a Backable Executive Campaign.

Based on the three sizes of PE firms, the Backable Executive "Incentives Budget" will likely be laid out like this:

Small-sized PE Firm budget:

Small PE firms typically acquire small businesses to lower-middle-market sized businesses. Highest "acquisition success" risk for the Backable Executive, with zero - to low monthly pay.

Commonly, we see firms in this group saying, "We want you to be entrepreneurial, put forward sweat equity, and take all the risk."

For that, if you source and close the acquisition, they will use a Lehman Formula or an alternative performance fee model. They will also pay you an hourly billable pay rate to conduct due diligence on a potential acquisition they are excited to pursue.

They will also provide equity in any acquisition you source commensurate with your role and responsibilities during the holding period and the opportunity to co-invest. They typically will look for Board Seat and industry roles and compensate you for this too.

Medium-sized PE Firm budget:

Medium PE firms typically acquire lower-middle-market to upper-middle-market sized businesses. Medium-level "acquisition success" risk for the Backable Executive... with low to medium monthly pay.

We commonly hear firms in this group say, "We see your true value, and we want some measure of exclusivity and a large portion of your hourly bandwidth. We still want you to be "intrapreneurially" driven, but we'll put more skin in the game and are willing to pay $10K to $30K per month."

If you source and close the acquisition, they will use a Lehman Formula or alternative performance fee model.

For example, incentives could include:

- Success fee equal to a Lehman Formula or 1% of total enterprise value.
- Equity worth .5% to 2.5%% of the invested capital.
- Opportunity for co-investment.
- An active chairman/board member's salary.

If you join the acquisition full-time:

- Salary and bonus (if dedicating 100% of professional time to business post-close).
- An employee stock ownership plan (ESOP) participation in the acquisition and earned additional equity.

Once an opportunity is identified, an executive's role depends on his or her preferences, level of desired involvement, and the nature of the situation (strength of management team, family dynamics, etc.).

PE Firms typically will support the Backable Executive taking one of the following roles:

- **CEO** - Traditional operational leader of a business.
- **Chairman** - Often strategic and M&A-focused but with no day-to-day operational responsibility.
- **Active Board Member** - Assists management with strategic projects in areas of expertise.

Large-sized PE Firm budget:

Large PE firms typically acquire upper-middle-market to very large-sized businesses. Lowest "acquisition success" risk for the Backable Executive… with high monthly pay.

The bigger the PE firm, the more likely they will say, "We want full exclusivity on all your available time for at least one year. For that commitment, we will pay you half of your last annual salary over the next year."

The rest of the compensation details for this level are very similar to those described in the medium tier.

It's worth noting that commission sharing occurs with the business developers who participate in deal flow sourcing. Like realtors, someone knows a seller, and someone else knows a buyer. The goal is to be the party with both buyer and seller in mind, but sometimes, just like realtors, you'll have to share.

You'll inevitably find a deal (a seller) from an investment banker, a sell-side advisor, a consultant, an attorney, an accountant, or even another PE making a referral asking to be incentivized for initially sourcing the lead and sharing it with you. So, here's a common sharing model to keep in mind.

There are three stages of work, each typically worth 1/3 of the total or to be negotiated in special cases.

1. The **Finder** secures fresh clientele for the firm.

This role demands extroversion, adaptability to new environments, exceptional communication skills, and the capacity to represent the company and its offerings adeptly within executive circles.

2. The **Minder** nurtures client relationships, engaging directly with the client's CFO.

Professional proficiency, effective communication abilities, insight into customer lifetime value, and the capacity to provide advisory support are essential in this role.

3. The **Grinder** is the person(s) making the deal decisions and closing the deal. They would typically collect 1/3 of the performance fee.

The Grinder can also be recognized as responsible for two of the three phases and, in such case, would collect 2/3 of the performance fee.

This is a straightforward way for determining how performance fees "could" be shared. The bottom line is that it's important to have these discussions up front, and to agree before all the work is done. Then align expectations regarding who is responsible for what. This way, when a performance fee is paid, there are no questions or confusion about how the split will occur.

We have provided this example for your consideration, just for reference, so you can compare what a well-crafted agreement might look like.

IN NO WAY SHOULD YOU IMPOSE THE BELOW ON ANY NEGOTIATION WITH ANY PE FIRM. It is simply provided here so you can prepare for what you might receive from a PE Firm.

SME / BACKABLE EXECUTIVE CONSULTING AGREEMENT:

- **Term:** Three months to one year.
- **Hourly rate:** $500, with a daily cap on the number of hours that can be billed.
- **Time commitment:** 10 hours per month = monthly cap of $5,000 and for each $2,000 increment thereafter.
- **Expenses:** $5,000 per month for travel (meals, lodging, air/ ground/rail transportation) and entertainment. No expense should be over $1,000 without prior approval, and no markup is allowed.
- Confidentiality agreements are required.
- Conflicts of interest are disclosed.
- All work products are the property of the PE firm.
- Independent contractor status.
- Discretionary cash bonus.

The Company shall award a discretionary cash bonus, capped at 1% of the total enterprise value, to the Advisor for significant services rendered, reflecting the Advisor's contribution or "value" as assessed solely by the Company. This bonus, recognizing the Advisor's efforts, may be distributed among multiple individuals who have significantly contributed, as decided solely by the Company. Furthermore, the Company reserves the right to disburse any awarded bonus in parts, along with any stipulations or prerequisites it deems appropriate, at its sole discretion.

FINDER AGREEMENT:

Services:

- Within the scope of this agreement, the consultant is tasked with aiding in the discovery, introduction, and assessment of potential acquisition targets and investment opportunities within the specified target industry sector. The services provided by the consultant will encompass:

    (i) developing investment theses and conducting market analysis,

    (ii) initiating contact with companies of interest, and,

    (iii) acting as an advisor during the due diligence process.

- The consultant will arrange the timing and locations for these services in collaboration with the Client, committing to the highest standards of professionalism, diligence, ethics, and care. This commitment is to ensure client satisfaction and to deliver the specialized knowledge needed for these tasks.

Deal Success Fees:

- The consultant and client will mutually decide and document which potential target(s) may qualify for a deal success fee (defined later). Only those targets approved in writing will be considered "eligible targets" for such a fee. It's important to note that the client is not obligated to pay a deal success fee unless there is a mutual written agreement with the consultant.

- Should the client finalize a deal with an eligible target within a year following their initial meeting arranged by the consultant (the "identification date"), the client agrees to promptly pay the consultant a deal success fee after each transaction closure. The "deal success fee" is defined as an equity-based incentive such as stock options, SARs, or profit interests in the eligible target or its post-closing parent entity equivalent to 1% of the cash paid by the client for the acquisition, funded solely by the client's equity financing. This fee applies only to the client's initial investment in an eligible target, excluding any follow-on investments. The fee will be fully vested at the time of issuance and structured to comply with all relevant tax and legal regulations. Furthermore, the client and consultant will explore opportunities for the consultant to continue involvement with the investment, potentially in management or advisory capacities.

- If the client is engaged in ongoing negotiations or due diligence with a prospective investment at the end of the specified year and closes the transaction within the following three months, this transaction will also qualify for the deal success fee as outlined in Section (a).

- Post-transaction, the client and consultant will consider additional opportunities for the consultant to support the eligible targets, possibly in management or board advisory roles. Any such compensation arrangements will be agreed upon separately.

Per Diem Fees:

- The client agrees to compensate the consultant at a rate of $500 per hour, with a daily limit of $4,000, for services provided to the client throughout the duration of the term. For activities related to the general target industry sector that cannot be directly linked to a specific transaction mutually acknowledged by both client and consultant, the annual maximum fees payable to the consultant will be capped at $50,000. Should there be a mutual written agreement between client and consultant to engage in services specific to a particular transaction, at that time, they will decide on an appropriate duration for the consultant's involvement in said transaction and establish a suitable daily fee cap for such services. Unless a different arrangement is agreed upon, fees are to be paid monthly in the following manner:

- The consultant will issue an invoice to the client within fifteen (15) days following the conclusion of each month. This invoice will detail the hours worked and services performed during the period, along with any reasonable documentation requested by the client for verification purposes.

Exclusivity:

- Throughout the term of this agreement, the consultant is prohibited from directly or indirectly suggesting or referring any target or eligible target to any third party or from offering advice or assistance in any manner concerning transactions involving a target unless the client has formally communicated through written notice its disinterest in that target.

- It is mutually understood and agreed that the consultant may refer targets to others if the acquisition of such targets involves an equity requirement of less than $50 million, except in cases where a target could complement an existing client platform or if the consultant and client decide together to invest in a target (defined as an "exempt target").

- However, it should be noted that if the consultant refers any target (excluding exempt targets) to another party or provides advice or assistance regarding transactions involving a target during the covered period, the consultant will forfeit the right to any deal success fee related to any transaction with such target, regardless of whether the Client has declared disinterest in writing.

- Moreover, if the consultant chooses to end this agreement or opts not to renew the engagement upon the client's request after its term concludes, the consultant will not be eligible for a deal success fee for any transactions finalized post-termination or after the engagement period.

As it relates to negotiating a Backable Executive Agreement with a PE firm, let me close this section with reminding you of what motivates the PE leadership the most:

As the Backable Executive (post-acquisition) are you focused on one of these three roles:

1. Taking a CXO role in the new acquisition and now focused on running the acquired business.
   This is valuable = Good.

2. Skipping a CXO role and instead serving as a chairmen/advisor over the acquisition while continuing to source and acquire bolt-ons.
   This is really valuable = Great.

3. Joining the PE firm full-time as an operating partner and/or serial acquisition hunter, focusing exclusively on making more acquisitions. Acquire a platform,

then acquire bolt-ons, and then repeat, again and again.
This is extremely valuable = Fantastic, Awesome... the PE firm will love it!

Depending on the answers to the above questions, PE firms are more motivated to incentivize the third option. "Golden handcuffs" are typically negotiated into the Backable Executive agreement to keep the BEST acquisition hunters engaged with the PE firm and ideally focused on becoming a serial acquisition hunter.

Addressing additional issues like:

- How much business development "cold calling support" will the Backable Executive need?
- How many SMEs will the Backable Executive require to manage acquisition due diligence during the campaign?
- How much investment is the Backable Executive committed to as part of the campaign?

Flushing these issues out during the negotiations will help align expectations and reduce friction as the acquisition-hunting campaign kicks into full execution mode.

As food for thought, we hear from many of our PE Clients (and the Executives they pay on a billable-hours basis) that this model is a good starting point:

- If an executive is used to a salary of $250K per year – they typically are paid $250/hour.
- If an executive is used to a salary of $350K per year – they typically are paid $350/hour.
- If an executive is used to a salary of $500K per year – they typically are paid $500/hour.

The following information graphic details several aspects of compensation and a general set of commercial terms that will be covered in most contract templates:

> Backable Executive Compensation Levers

---

1 **Payment for Billable Hours with Cap Limits:**

What we hear from many of our PE Clients and the Executives that they pay billable hours to—is this:

- If an Executive is used to a salary of $250K per year – they should be paid $250/hour for each billable hour.
- If an Executive is used to a salary of $350K per year – they should be paid $350/hour for each billable hour.
- If an Executive is used to a salary of $500K per year – they should be paid $500/hour for each billable hour.
- If an Executive is used to a salary over $500K per year be prepared for up to $1,000/hour for each billable hour.

Or a Monthly Retainer / Salary Approach:

Low Zero cash up front

Middle $15K per month

High Up to half the Executive's previous annual Salary

A Draw/Loan against a Success Fee

---

2 **Expense Coverage**

3 **Discretionary Bonuses**

4 **Deal Success Fee for an Acquisition Lead:**

Transaction fee @ 1% of Acquisition...

or the Lehman Formula:
The 1st million is at a 5% fee.
the 2nd is at 4%,
the 3rd is at 3%,
the 4th is at 2%,
the 5th million (and beyond) is at 1%.
Up to a cap of a total of $1 million in fees.

5 **Opportunity to Re/Co Invest**

6 **Exclusivity Commitment**

7 **Time Commitment**

8 **Incentive Units "Post Acquisition"**

9 **CXO, Board or Advisory Compensation Package "Post Acquisition"**

10 **ESOP participation and/or additional earned equity in the acquisition**

Some Investment Incentivization Questions you may want to ask:

- What is your PE firm's investment model for executives who serve as acquisition hunters?
- Do you charge management fees for which I would be responsible if I invest, or am I included in the management team with no expenses charged?
- What is the equity structure? Please explain how I get to the different levels of return that you've modeled.
- Do you have a preferred yield on equity investments?
- Show me your base cap, upside, and downside at different return levels.
- Typical shareholder agreements govern the prioritization of liquidity events and in this order:
    1. Debt
    2. Equity
    3. Preferred yield (if there is one)
    4. B Pool
    5. C Pool

Rarely are the above ever negotiable; only the number of the shares you may receive.

Equity structures are typically well-set in stone, but it doesn't hurt to ask for an explanation if something is not spelled out in the agreement.

Sometimes, you can get a PE firm to add a provision for dilution protection, as the PE leadership doesn't want management to worry about whether they'll have to fund additional equity. In this scenario, if an acquisition requires equity, the PE firm will give the shares that were held aside for management so that they maintain their ownership percentage without being diluted.

That said, if PE leadership asks you to write a check as part of an acquisition, take it as an honor. They usually only ask those they respect to invest in this scenario. This is also a unique opportunity to invest with highly sophisticated and very successful investors — a rare opportunity most executives never get exposed to.

Play the long game. Of course, get as much as you can from these negotiations now, but DO NOT forget this PE partnering opportunity has long-term financial implications. If at exit (sale of any of the acquisitions you sourced and received equity for) you are not yet ready to retire... DON'T completely cash out.

Instead, roll forward some of your proceeds and keep the money working for you. A good suggestion is to cash out 70 to 75% of every dollar you're paid and leave in 25 to 30%. Based on your taxation scenario, you and your accountant should determine the right percentage.

Always watch for the opportunity to reinvest in a company and management team in which you believe. When the company is sold again, you can get a second bite of the apple, which, in certain situations, can be meaningful in comparison to the first bite. For instance, let's say you decide to roll 30% forward, and three-to-five years later, the company is sold again, generating a 4X MOIC. In this instance, you have effectively quadrupled the capital you rolled forward and created another lucrative liquidity event, often larger than the first. While all investments carry risk, investing alongside private equity and management teams you know and trust can be quite appealing compared to the stock market. The story's moral is that you should always watch for a second bite of the apple if you truly believe in the company and its mission.

Of course, this assumes the company still has a growth runway and will keep improving as it grows under its new ownership. This doesn't always happen, but you know this company better than anyone; so, reinvest if you believe in it.

Let's say that you (as a serial acquisition hunter) have identified multiple platforms and bolt–ons, and now, three-to-five years later, they are all heading towards short-term exits. Using the multiplication factor of what was used in the previous example can generate massive generational wealth.

Here's some valuable food for thought as you consider your next move.

These are some questions your spouse, family, friends, and peers are going to ask you:

Should you just work for a public company and keep climbing the corporate ladder?

Is it better to be a small fish in a very large pond (one of thousands, like large public companies) or a large fish in a very small pond (one of 50 to 100, typical of most PE acquisition targets)?

Should you leave the comfort of working as a CEO and become a direct part of working for or supporting PE acquisitions? Isn't the first safer than the latter?

What's more important: chasing titles and a secure paycheck or the opportunity to generate generational wealth through investing alongside PE in the private market, with the ability to quickly build a very large private portfolio?

Before you fully retire, you can diversify rather than settle for the smooth, safe path to retirement. Yes, you can stay in the big company lane and slowly, safely sail into the harbor on a big boat, but your pedigree has opened a new door for you to leverage your expertise in a way no large company will appreciate as much as a PE firm will.

Few people make below seven figure salaries in the Fortune 500 C-suite world as a percentage of the total employee base. Compare that to private equity-backed, middle-market companies, and you might be surprised. A six-figure employee in middle management in a Fortune 500 can be a seven-figure employee in the middle market, once you factor in base, bonus, stock incentives, and ability to invest alongside their PE peers/sponsor.

Besides, is the risk of working in the PE world any worse than getting laid off by a large public company? Security is fleeting, an illusion, like a puff of smoke. Why wait for a new CEO or board member to disrupt your world? Disrupt yourself, before someone else gets to do it to you first.

The first year you transition to working with PE could be a serious salary hit, but if you've been investing all along the way (to where you are now), you can very likely afford it. The subsequent years are going to more than make up for it.

Besides, the learning curve you will benefit from and the excitement you will have in this new entrepreneurial (or really "intrapreneurial") opportunity will be beneficial from a career perspective but more so, extremely exciting. Just ask any PE founder who took the risk of leaving corporate America and then made the plunge to join the dynamic, fast-paced world of PE, eventually even starting their own PE firm.

"We are stubborn on vision. We are flexible on details."
Jeff Bezos, Founder and Former CEO of Amazon

A couple more closing thoughts:

PE moves at a very fast pace. The leaders who join up with private equity for the first time need to understand the pace of the race typically changes from the corporate world to the PE world.

It's worth understanding that as an athlete gets older, speed changes. Picture how fast a Formula 1 race car driver transitions from driving go-karts to NASCAR to Formula 1. It's typically about a 10-to-15-year process. How fast they cycle out of driving for Formula 1 is about a 5-to-10-year lifecycle. Safety and technology have made these racing careers last longer. However, the winningest drivers are usually the youngest, and after about five years, their winning tends to start fading away.

When they first arrive, new drivers are amazed at the speed and pace of change compared to all other racing styles. Soon, they acclimate; they learn to eat, exercise, and rest better. As a result of better care, their lifestyle and income are typically substantially better than before they joined the fast-paced life of Formula 1.

Much is the same in the world of PE. In the early days, it will be a different game than the corporate world to which you are accustomed. You will notice a significant pace difference, and the track will seem very small since people cover greater distances in PE much faster.

It's this way because the internal rate of return (IRR) time clock is ticking, hours are longer, and time is recognized as way more valuable. You will hear it a lot — every minute is calculated and closely managed. TIME is the PE leader's most valuable asset! Dedication to productivity is a close second. So, you must learn how to manage wins and losses much faster.

You'll get a big high when you make an acquisition or exit and deep lows when you lose acquisitions you've invested substantial time into. My advice is just like a Formula 1 race team: at the end of the day, NO MATTER WHAT, WIN OR LOSE... get over it and get ready for the next race, because just like in a world-class PE firm, more race opportunities are going to be coming at you fast.

This is also why it's so important you pick the right PE team to join or support. The right team will help you manage stress and frustration and will coach you to manage at this faster pace. When you are properly aligned, and everyone sees that it's true, the team enjoys and benefits from the faster pace of pushing and pulling each other forward, making them all better athletes.

Athletes love being around (playing with and/or competing against) the best in their field. They train harder, they learn faster, and they practice more, even though they may be at the top of their game and already considered one of the best. They do so because they want to be the very best, and they understand that's what it takes to be world champions.

Maybe they are at the top of their game and are considered the best in their field. They do so because they want to be the best, and they understand that's what it takes to be world champions.

One of the key "champion" stats in PE is double-digit organic growth within three years. The good news is that you're not on your own. Most PE Firms build great teams to help make this happen, with specialists to help find acquisition opportunities, conduct due diligence, complete financial modeling, draft NDAs and agreements, evaluate operations, sales, and marketing, plan for integrations, and much more.

There are analysts for every need and plentiful, established relationships with law firms, accountants, investment bankers, HR experts, SME consultants, head-hunters, and more. This is a great place to learn how to build out your own deal team, source the best (over time), and begin building your own SME network.

Bottom line PE leaders are very savvy investors and represent limited partners who are also savvy investors. They bring a wealth of expertise and a great learning opportunity with a depth of networking contacts that can expand your world of opportunities.

Once you fully retire, your credibility to become a trusted advisor serving as a CEO coach will be very high! Check out the organization Vistage or CEO Coaching International. Look at the world-class roster of leaders these organizations have serving as CEO coaches. They're having a blast, making a very nice income for working limited hours, and even getting more equity in the firms they support.

Acknowledgments

The following books inspired me:

Think and Grow Rich by Napolean Hill

How to Win Friends and Influence People by Dale Carnegie

Good to Great by Jim Collins

Scaling Up by Verne Harnish

Make Big Happen by Mark Moses

Buy & Build CEO by Ted Clark

The Private Equity Playbook by Adam Coffey

A Cartoon Lovers Guide to Private Equity by David Toll

Exit Rich by Michelle Seiler Tucker and Sharon Lechter

Backable by Suneel Gupta

About the Author

Patrick Ropella is a visionary entrepreneur and executive leader with more than 35 years of unparalleled experience in founding and steering a globally leading executive search firm, a private equity services firm, and an information research firm, as presented at: www.ropella360.com

As well, Patrick has established Ropella Equity Ventures as his own PE investment firm. Patrick also builds high-end custom homes and creates a wide variety of beautiful art "in his free time," through his own art gallery at: www.ropellaart.com

Throughout his distinguished career, he has been a driving force in C-Suite leader sourcing, assessment, and development, as well in succession and exit planning, business assessment, and value creation for many mid-market private equity-backed companies.

He has successfully contributed to the growth of major global corporate technology organizations such as DOW, General Electric, BASF, Georgia Pacific, SONY, Tyco Electronics, Nike, Clorox, PPG, Revlon, Baxter Labs, Johnson & Johnson, Shell, and many more. He has also helped hundreds of startups and mid-sized companies grow from good to great.

Patrick has perfected the art of executive search as presented in his best-selling book *The Right Hire*, and has developed a system for providing very high-quality client experiences, delivered very fast through Ropella 360's proprietary Smart Search System. Patrick has also created a large IP portfolio of web-based software and calculators for the ROI of Hiring, Comparing Compensation Packages, and more.

As Ropella 360 looks to the future, Patrick is now leveraging his 35+ year global network (counted in the millions) and his unique experiences to serve as an advisor and/or strategic partner for private equity and other investment firms. He contributes his expertise on the buy and sell sides, as well serving Backable Executives, conducting SME searches, and board seat searches for a long list of high-net-worth clients.

Ropella 360 stands as a leading "SEARCH" firm, serving as SuperConnectors, while heavily focused on the chemicals, consumer products, and general industrials sectors. The firm is now expanding into robotics, AI, and space exploration.

Ropella 360's commitment to the future is exemplified through innovative approaches, such as connecting A-player, Level 5/Transformational leaders via our proprietary Deal Flow Accelerators campaigns, and positioning Ropella 360 as a trailblazer in reshaping private equity growth.

As the author of *The Right Hire* and now *The Pathways to Private Equity Partnerships*, Patrick's C-suite and investor insights are also featured in hundreds of publications worldwide, in multiple languages, solidifying his reputation as a thought leader in the realms of business and investment. As he navigates the remaining years of his career, Patrick remains dedicated to building the future of companies with a focus on unparalleled leadership, innovation development, and focused vision casting.

People. Platforms. Perspectives.

❯ The Ropella 360 Suite
Your own personal SuperConnector resource... providing SEARCH Services for:

People
The Right Executives

Identifying A-players & Level 5 transformational leaders as:

- Board Members
- C-Suite Executives
- Key Leaders & Team Builders
- PE Leadership
- Interim SMEs & Consultant

Platforms
The Right Company

Partnering with founders, innovators, and investors on:

- Sourcing Backable Execs
- Buy-Side Deal Flow
- Sell-Side Transactions
- Investment Possibilities

Perspectives
The Right Information

Directing XCAVATE Search Strategy for:

- Company List Building
- Executive List Building
- Sell-Side Transactions
- List Sorting And Prioritizing

WE DO THE DIGGING, SO YOU DON'T HAVE TO

UNCONVENTIONAL RESEARCH SYSTEM

Our proprietary system blends the use of Military Intelligence techniques with our 15-plus years of experience serving world-class Executive Search Firms.

"To know what you know and what you do not know, that is true knowledge." –Confucius

We are wise enough to know we don't know everything; therefore, we utilize our proprietary **UNCONVENTIONAL RESEARCH SYSTEM** to ensure we leave no data unmined.

We provide candidate lists for **EXECUTIVE SEARCH CONSULTANTS** for their clients who may be tired of paying for overseas sourced-lists that lack the quality they deserve.

OUR LISTS *result in a...*

80% HIRE RATE WITHIN THE FIRST 200 CANDIDATES.

We provide candidate lists for corporate **HIRING TEAMS** who wish to do their own recruiting.

Our **BRAND PROMISE GUARANTEE** *is...*

5 INTERVIEWS / PER / **100** CANDIDATES **GUARANTEED** OR WE'LL ADD *ANOTHER 50* FOR *FREE*

We support **PRIVATE EQUITY FIRMS** by providing lists of subject mater experts (SME) in their thesis focus, and lists of potential off-market acquisition targets within the private sector.

Our **UNCONVENTIONAL RESEARCH SYSTEM** *provides...*

Laser-like precision to find exactly what you're looking for, whether it be **SUBJECT MATTER EXPERTS** or **POTENTIAL ACQUISITIONS**.

📞 850.610.7321   ✉ SERVICE@XCAVATE.COM   🌐 XCAVATE.COM